FUNDAMENTAL PRINCI

PRINCIPLES OF GAMES	PRINCIPLES OF LOVE
Competition *Opposing teams* *Opponents*	*No Competition* *Everyone is on the same team* *Partners*
A Winner *A Loser*	*Everyone Always Wins* *No One Ever Loses*
Scoreboard *Keeps score* *Earn points when you score* *Based on what you do*	*No Scoreboard* *Doesn't keep score* *There are no points to earn* *Every expression of Love is maximal*
Rules *Restrictions, limitations* *You can be in the wrong* *By breaking the rules* *"Follow the rules"*	*No Rules to Break* *Love is unlimited* *Love is never wrong* *Love is Free* *"Do what you want to do"*
Referees *Supervise and enforce rules* *Make judgments* *Reward and punish behavior*	*No Referees* *No supervisors* *No judgments* *No punishments*
Attached to a Specific Outcome *Trying to GET something* *Goal is to win* *"Play to win!"* *"I'm in it to win it"*	*Unattached to a Specific Outcome* *Not trying to GET anything* *Goal is to enjoy the experience* *"Have fun!"* *"I'm in it for the experience"*
Time Limits *Begins* *Ends* *Takes timeouts*	*Transcends Time* *No beginning* *No ending* *Love takes no breaks or timeouts*
Space Limits *Can only be played in certain places* *With certain people*	*Transcends Space* *Can experience Love anywhere* *With anyone*
Conformity	*Creative Expression*
Fun if you win *Not fun if you lose*	*Fun for Everyone* *Fun all the time*

Love

IS *NOT* A

GAME

A Manual for Loving Relationships

Author
Editor
Cover
Design Layout
Na'Im Najieb

THIS BOOK IS DEDICATED TO YOU

ACKNOWLEDGEMENTS

Thank You

4

TABLE OF CONTENTS

PART 2 - THE TWO CURRICULUMS 43

PART 1
OPEN YOUR MIND
Are You Ready?

**This Manual contains ideas.
These ideas are powerful.**

They will give you an entirely different way of
Seeing and thinking about Love and relationships.

What is Part 1 of this Manual about?

The first part of this Manual is your Initiation into
The Thought System and ideas you will be learning and using.
You will be asked to participate in this process.
You will be shown the value and simplicity of the ideas.
You will be given exercises that will prepare you
And your relationship for what's to come.
***This part lays the groundwork for
The curriculum contained in this Manual.***

IMPORTANT!

*You do not have to believe the ideas.
You do not have to accept the ideas.
You do not have to welcome the ideas.*

*Some of the ideas may be hard to believe.
Some of the ideas you may find disagreeable.
Some of the ideas you may actively resist.*

None of this matters whatsoever.

You are only asked to **USE** the ideas.

*If you use the ideas,
They will have meaning to you.*

The results of using the ideas will show you that they are True.

INSTRUCTIONS
This is a Manual for Loving Relationships

These are the instructions for reading this Manual.

Why instructions?
Isn't this supposed to be an "Introduction"?

No, **INSTRUCTIONS!**
This is a Manual, not a novel. This book is instructional.
This Manual is not to be confused with a "self-help" book that you
Passively read and then forget about.

This is not a book you just read, this is a book you DO.

This is a Manual for Loving Relationships
This Manual will offer you another way to look at Love.
This Manual will tell you what to do to have Love
Constantly flow in your relationship.
When Love is not flowing,
It will tell you why it isn't flowing, and what to do to correct it.

This Manual will not go into detailed explanations about
WHY you should do what it tells you to do.
If there is a problem, it will be identified,
And the solution will be offered you.
You can choose to use it or not.

This Manual is about you, your partner, and your relationship.
This is not a novel, and it is certainly not a game.

The Truth in this Manual is ready for you.

The question is:

Are you ready for the Truth?

Rules for Using This Manual

Three Rules

First Rule for Using This Manual:

- If you are in a relationship, read this Manual **with your partner.**
  - **DO NOT** read this Manual without your partner.
  - The only reason you should read this Manual by yourself is if you are single.

Why?

This Manual is for partners.
This Manual is to be read and applied *together*.
This Manual is not written for one person
Who wants to improve the relationship alone.
It is for two *willing* people who want to
Improve their relationship together.

So, if you are currently in a relationship,
And you have no intentions to read this Manual with your partner,
Or your partner is not willing to read this Manual with you –
Do both of you a favor,

DON'T READ THIS MANUAL.

It will do more harm than good.

Why?

Because there is only one result of applying the principles in this Manual –

Growth.

If you are the only one in the relationship who is committed to growth,
You will grow while your partner remains stagnant.
You will feel unequally yoked in your relationship,
And you will resent your partner.
In other words…

You will outgrow your partner.

Remember:

Your relationship is a partnership.
If you are going to Progress, you will Progress together.
If you are going to Grow, you will Grow together.
If you are going to Learn, you will Learn together.
If you are going to Heal, you will Heal together.
If you are going to experience True Love,
You will experience True Love together.

Second Rule for Using This Manual:
- Buy 2 notebooks, one for you and one for your partner.
  - Use these notebooks solely for applying the curriculum in this Manual, doing the assignments and taking notes.

Third Rule for Using This Manual:

Apply the concepts in this book together
IMMEDIATELY.

When there is something to do together
DO IT.

When there is a conversation to have
HAVE IT.

When there is a decision to make
MAKE IT.

Because...

If not now,
When?

If not you,
Who?

If not this relationship,
Which one?

Start now.
This is not a game.

BEFORE YOU BEGIN...

Before you read this Manual, ask yourself these questions:

- *Am I willing to admit that I do not know what Love is or how to do it all the time?*

- *Am I willing to admit that the way I have been taught to practice relationships does not serve my Happiness?*

- *Am I willing to admit that I've been programed to think about Love and relationships in a certain way?*

- *Am I willing to admit that this programming is anti-Happiness?*

- *Am I willing to admit that this programming is the source of fear and upset in relationships?*

- *Am I willing to admit that the results of listening to this programming are dysfunctional relationships?*

- *Do I recognize that I've been programmed since birth?*

- *Do I recognize that this programming has been detrimental to my understanding of Love?*

- *Do I recognize that this programming has been designed to block True Love from my awareness?*

- *Do I want to get past my programming?*

- *If there were a curriculum that would show me another way of looking at this programming, and help me to deprogram myself, would I do it?*

- *If I am currently in a relationship, am I willing to join with my partner in this curriculum?*

- *Am I willing to take a stand for Love with my partner?*

- *Am I willing to dedicate our relationship to Love, and only Love?*

If you answered yes to all of these questions, and yes, *all of them* –
You are ready to continue using this Manual.

Turn the page.

Love?

Love does not attack
Love does not change
Love does not compete
Love does not play games

Love cannot be threatened
Love cannot be hurt
Love Heals all things
Love fills all hearts

Love is not a feeling
Love is not different things
Love is always One
Love is always the same

Love is not romance
Love is not flowers and cards
Love is what created you
Love is what you are

Love is beyond space
Love is beyond time
Love is beyond bodies
Love is beyond minds

Love does not fight
Love does not abuse
Love always wins
Love never loses

Love does not argue
Love takes no breaks
Love is real
Love is not fake

Love is not a rehearsal
Love is not a drill
Love is always Live
Love is the Real Deal

Love does not take
Love does not compare
Love only gives
Love always shares

Love is Freedom
Love is Truth
Love is willing
Love does what it wants to do

Love does not hurt
Love causes no pain
Love always wins
And Love plays no games

You deserve to be Happy.
You deserve total Love and to be totally Loved.
You deserve Totally Fulfilling relationships with everyone in your life.
Your inheritance is Love, Peace, and Totally Fulfilling relationships.
Period.

PURPOSE OF THIS MANUAL

What is the Purpose of This Manual?

- The purpose of this Manual is to save you and your partner time.
  - The time that is wasted in heartbreak, upset, confusion, distress, depression, etc.
- The purpose of this Manual is to return your common sense to you about Love and relationships. *Why?*
  - Because we are living in a time of *common nonsense* about Love and relationships.
- The purpose of this Manual is to teach you to identify your insane programming. *Why?*
  - So you can make a conscious choice to refuse to follow it.
- The purpose of this Manual is Healing.
  - Using your relationship as the means to Heal from your emotional wounds.
- The purpose of this Manual is to teach you how to have Totally Fulfilling relationships.
- The purpose of this Manual is to teach you the thought system of Love.
  - You will learn how Love thinks and operates.
- The purpose of this Manual is to teach you the thought system of the program (aka fear).
  - You will learn how the program thinks and operates.

PREMISE OF THIS MANUAL

Love is Everything, fear is Nothing

There is nothing original about the content and message of this Manual.
The content is Love, and the message is Love.

The only thing that is original is the form it is being presented in.
This Manual gives you a basic understanding of
The *thought system* (or curriculum) of Love.
It also exposes the thought system of the program (fear).

The thought system of Love offered in this Manual
Is derived from a book entitled:
A Course In Miracles

You do not need to be familiar with
A Course In Miracles in order to benefit from this Manual.
A Course In Miracles is not special.
It is just one form of the Universal Curriculum of Love.

This Manual applies the curriculum of Love
Specifically to your relationship.

Premises
The ideas contained in this Manual are built on a few basic premises.
You should be aware of these premises,
Because they are the foundation for everything.

Fundamental Ideas
- **Love is Everything**
    - o Love is the only thing that matters.
    - o Love is real.
- **Fear is Nothing**
    - o Fear is the blocking of Love.
    - o Fear is an illusion.
- **You Come from Love**
    - o Love created you.
- **Love is an Infinitely Intelligent Internal Force**
    - o When you learn to identify it, you can tap into it at any time.
    - o Love will always guide you truly.
- **You Were NOT born with fear**
    - o You were programmed to fear.
    - o Fear was taught to you.
- **You Want Only to Love and to be Loved**
    - o You do not want fear in any form.
- **There Are Only Two Experiences to Choose From**
    - o Love or fear.
- **Fear can be Deprogrammed**

- o With the right tools and training, fear will no longer have any effect on you or your relationship.
- **You Have the Power of Decision**
  - o Love is a decision.
  - o Fear is a decision.
- **Love Does Not Need to be Learned**
  - o Love needs to be remembered.
- **Every Problem in your Relationship Comes from Blocking (or Forgetting) Love**
- **The Solution to Every Problem in Your Relationship Comes When You Remember Love**

PROMISE OF THIS MANUAL
The Truth

This Manual is unlike any relationship book
You have ever read or heard about.

What does this Manual promise?

- It promises to teach you how to identify and remove the barriers to Love in your relationship
- It promises to offer you another way to look at Love and relationships
- It promises to show you why relationships fail
  - o What **NOT TO DO** in your relationship
- It promises to show you how to have a Healthy relationship
  - o What **TO DO** in your relationship
- It promises to offer you a practical curriculum you can apply to absolutely ANY relationship
- It promises to save you time

PRACTICE AND PARTICIPATION IN THIS MANUAL
Play Your Part
If You Use the Ideas, You Will See That They Work

This is your part.

The purpose, premise, and promise of this Manual will only
Be Truly Helpful in your relationship
To the extent that you and your partner do this one thing –

DO IT!

Again, this book is a Manual.
If you want the results it promises,
Your practice and participation are required.

You do not have to believe, accept, or welcome the ideas it contains.
The only thing that is asked is that you USE them.
APPLY the ideas in your relationship with your partner **TOGETHER.**

If you use the ideas,
You will see that they work.

What is required of you to benefit from this Manual?

Let's start with what is NOT required of you.
It is not required that you know what Love is and how to do it all the time.
It is only required that you want to - that you want only Love.

What does this mean?
It means that it is also required that you decide that you no longer want
The insane programming you were taught about Love and relationships.
You cannot have both at the same time.
You cannot have Light and darkness, Love and fear,
Or Sanity and insanity at the same time.
You have to give up one to have the other.
You will be shown how to identify both, so your decision becomes easy,
And your relationship remains Loving.

PRINCIPLES IN THIS MANUAL
We're Talking About YOU...
And You, and You, and You

The word *"you"* is used very often in this Manual.
Why?
Because this Manual is for you, and about you.

"You" refers to *you* the reader and your partner at the same time.

This Manual is based on Universal Principles.
It does not deal with theory.
What are Universal Principles?

Universal Principles are principles that are True.
They are True for everyone, and they are True all the time.
At no point do Universal Principles start being True or stop being True.
They refer to everyone, and every relationship.
Everyone is the same.

How can you tell if something is NOT a Universal Principle?

If at any point the principle can be threatened by anything,
Or there is even one exception found in any person,
Or in any relationship at ANY time,
It is **NOT** True.

This is why you will not find anything in this Manual that mentions:

- "Most relationships…"
- "Most people…"
- "Most men…"
- "Most women…"
- "Gender roles" in relationships
- "Case studies" about relationships
- "Research" about relationships

Why?

Because if it is not True for everyone ALL the time,
It is NOT True.
Therefore it is of no value to you.

So remember this while you are reading:

When it comes to the Truth about Love,
Everyone is the same.
The Truth is True for everyone.

Throughout this Manual you will see different principles featured
As follows:

"TRUTH PRINCIPLE"
When you see this, it means this principle is Universally True.

"LOVE PRINCIPLE"
This principle operates ONLY in Love's thought system.

"PROGRAM PRINCIPLE"
This principle operates ONLY in the program's thought system.

PRESENTATION OF THIS MANUAL
Three Parts

This Manual is presented in three parts:

Part 1
Opening Your Mind

"Are you ready?"

The Purpose of Part 1 is:
- To establish that this book is a Manual and not a romance novel.
- To establish that the purpose of this Manual is to offer ideas.
- To prepare your mind for the ideas contained in this Manual.
- To give you practical tools to use in your relationship.

(You are currently reading part 1).

Part 2
The Curriculum

"What is Love?"
"What is the program?"

The Purpose of Part 2 is:
- To introduce you to your two teachers
- To explore the two entirely different thought systems they offer.
- To explain the thought system and principles of Love.
- To expose the insane thought system and fearful principles of the program.
- To clarify the ideas the program uses to confuse you about Love.

Part 3
Relationship Matters

"What about...?"

The Purpose of Part 3 is:
- To look at common relationship topics and themes.
- To ask those questions that often come up in relationships.
- To give you answers from BOTH thought systems covered in Part 2.
  - *How does Love see this?*
  - *How does the program see this?*
- To give you another way of looking at things.
- To start a conversation.
  - Explore each other's thoughts on these topics.

How do you get the most from this Manual?

You and your partner will get the most from this Manual
When you follow it as it is laid out:
Step by step, page by page, chapter by chapter and part by part.

PURIFICATION PROCESS
Everything Unloving Will Come up to be Released

FAIR WARNING

By following this curriculum,
Your relationship will go through what's called:
"The Purification Process"

What does this mean?

The purification process is a stage in your relationship where
Everything unpleasant will come up.

Why is it coming up?

It's coming up in order to be Healed.
It's coming up in order to be released forever.

The question is not IF it will come,

The question is:
"WHEN?"
This is not being said to scare you.
This is being said to prepare you.

The fact is, when you clean house,
What do you have to target?
The dirt.

When you set the goal to Purify your relationship to have only
Love, Peace, and Happiness.
You have to look at all of the guilt, fear, and conflict first.
Why?
So you can decide that you no longer want it -
TOGETHER.

When there are short periods of disturbance in your Love and Peace -
Just know that there is nothing unusual about this happening.

Here's the Good news!

Those periods will not last long.
You will be given the tools you need to get through any disturbance
QUICKLY.

As long as you continue to Join in Love, and use the tools –
Nothing will have the power to threaten your relationship.

Remember:
You and your partner are ALWAYS on the same team.

The program (fear) *will* come up in your relationship.
Before, it would destroy your relationship,
Because you didn't know what it was.
Now, you and your partner will have the tools
You need in order to deal with it.

You are being told about this now so you do not think that
Something is wrong with you or your relationship
When you experience disturbance.

These things happen.

Partners Use This Manual
You and Your Partner Are the Same

This Manual is written from the standpoint that
You and your partner are the same.
You are the same because you both come from Love.
And you are the same because you have both been programmed.

Programmed how?
You have been programmed to forget Love.
You have been programmed to use your relationship to hurt yourself.

What about Love?
Now, you do not need to learn anything about Love -
Because Love is what you are.

You do need to **unlearn** the programming that was taught to you.
This is called **deprogramming.**
You are not immune to the program – yet.
You must Heal in order to prevent yourself from being infected by it.
You will use your Loving relationship to Heal and deprogram yourself.

Programming Exposed in This Manual
Deprogramming

You have been emotionally wounded.
This is not a theory, this is a fact.

Why is this so?
Because you have been programmed,
And the result of this programming is ALWAYS
Emotional pain and emotional wounds.
It is the same as growing up in a place where the air is polluted.
Everyone breathes the same air, so everyone is sick.

How do you Heal?
The first step in Healing is to admit that you are hurt.
The next step is to not want the hurt anymore.
The next step is to ask for help,
And the final step is to receive the help.

It seems simple right?

If you are hurt, you ask for help, and you receive help.
Here's where the program tries to trick you.
It wants you to think that you can
DO IT BY YOURSELF.

This is the oldest trick in the program's book.

The program also wants you to think that you can focus on the hurt,
And by focusing on it – you can let it go.
This is impossible.

You must focus on the Love.

The Love between you and your partner.

The content of this curriculum is for you to *Join,*
Especially in the presence of deep fear.

Your relationship is the means by which you will Heal.

You will use your relationship to deprogram yourself.

What is Deprogramming?

Deprogramming is ***unlearning.***

You don't need to learn anything new.
You need to *unlearn* the program's insane ideas and lessons.
Those insane ideas are **blocking Love** from your awareness.
As you unlearn those ideas, your mind will automatically align with Love.

How do you unlearn?

Deprogramming or unlearning follows the same principles of learning.

What is the mother of all learning?

Repetition
Repetition
Repetition

How were you programmed?

Through repetition.

The program's insane ideas about Love were repeated to you
Over and over and over in different forms,
Until you finally adopted them as YOUR ideas.

By repeating Love's ideas,
We are using the principle of repetition in the service of Love.

There is a lot of repetition in this Manual.
This Manual contains a lot of repetition.
It repeats itself a lot.

Why?

All of the ideas contained in this Manual are connected,
So they will be repeated to reinforce their importance.

Repetition will *save you time* in the deprogramming process.

PROCEED WITH THIS MANUAL
You are Prepared

You know the ***Purpose*** of this Manual.

You know the ***Premises*** it is based on.

You know what it ***Promises*** you.

You know you are asked to ***Play your Part,***

And ***Practice and Participate*** in the ***Process.***

You know it is based on Universal ***Principles.***

You know how it will be ***Presented*** to you.

You know your relationship will undergo a ***Purification Process.***

You know this Manual is written for ***Partners,***

And that you and your ***Partner*** are the same.

You know you will encounter the ***Program.***

You are **Prepared.**

You May Proceed.

CHAPTER 1
YOUR RELATION*SHIP*
A Vehicle

In this chapter, we're going to take a look at relationships.

What are Relationships?
What are Relationships not?

We often have the wrong ideas about relationships and what they're for -
Especially relationships with an intimate partner.
Let's review some of these popular but erroneous ideas,
So we can get an idea of what your relationship is NOT for,
And what your partner is NOT for.

If you use your relationship or your partner
For any of the following reasons,
You will hurt yourself.

WHAT IS YOUR RELATIONSHIP NOT?

A Healthy Relationship is NOT any of the following:
- A distraction from your life
- Something that completes you
  - You enter a relationship already complete
- Something you use to hurt yourself or each other
- A source of:
  - Guilt
  - Fear
  - Strain
  - Distress
  - Drama
  - Pain
  - Misery
- Something that will stay the same and not change
  - Nothing on the level of form stays the same
  - Your relationship WILL change form
- Something that hinders your progress toward your personal goals

WHAT IS YOUR PARTNER NOT?

Your partner is NOT any of the following:
- Your Entertainment
    - o   Your partner is not in the relationship to entertain you
- Your Counselor
    - o   Your partner is not your therapist
- Your servant
    - o   Your partner is not in the relationship to please you
- Responsible for your feelings
    - o   Your partner is not in the relationship to "make" you Happy
- Going to make you feel "complete"
    - o   No one can complete you
    - o   You and your partner are already complete
- Going to stay the same and not change
    - o   Everyone changes all the time
- Your only source of Love
    - o   Love is not limited to your partner or your relationship
- Your opponent
    - o   You are partners, not rivals
    - o   You are on the same team all the time

If you are expecting anyone to fulfill these imagined needs in you,
You will hurt yourself with that relationship.
Even if you both make a commitment to fulfill these things for each other,
It will not work, because it is an impossible task.

WHAT IS YOUR PARTNER FOR?

What Do You Do In A Healthy Relationship With Your Partner?

In a Healthy Relationship, you and your partner:
- Join on a common goal
- Join on a common curriculum
- Trust each other totally and completely
- Commit to the content of Love in the relationship
    - o   Do not commit to a certain form of relationship
- Know that you are not going to understand each other fully all the time
    - o   You don't need to understand each other fully to Love each other fully

- Make a point to show your Appreciation for each other as often as possible
- Free each other
- Support each other's Peace

WHAT ARE LOVING RELATIONSHIPS FOR?
How does Love use Relationships?

Love uses relationships for **Healing.**
Love uses your relationships to support your Peace of mind.
Relationships that are devoted to Love
Are a place of rest and rejuvenation for your Soul.

THE TWO KEYS TO A HEALTHY RELATIONSHIP
A Common Goal and a Common Curriculum

There are two key ingredients that are needed in any Loving relationship.
What is their purpose?
Having these two keys will ensure your relationship will be
Healthy, Happy, and Loving.

The great thing about these two ingredients
Is that you can add them to your relationship at any time,
And they will work.

What are these two main ingredients?

1. **A Common Goal**
2. **A Common Curriculum**

Without these ingredients, your relationship will eventually deteriorate,
And you will grow apart.

What is a Common Goal?

Having a Common Goal starts by asking yourself
And your partner these questions:

What is the purpose of our relationship?
What is our relationship for?
Why are we together?

This is one of the conversations you will have later on,
In the chapter: *"Setting the Goal"*.

What is the importance of a Common Goal?

Having a Common Goal is the same as having a common destination.
A relationship is a vehicle, and when you get into a vehicle with someone,
You want to be sure you both agree on where you are going.

An important thing to remember about the Goal and Purpose of
Your relationship is this:

Focus on the content you want in the relationship,
Do not focus on the form.

We will discuss form and content later.

WHAT IS A CURRICULUM?
A System

A curriculum is a *thought system*.
Your thought system becomes your *belief system*.
Your belief system becomes your *guidance system*
A belief system also becomes your *value system.*
Your value system eventually becomes your *identity*,
Because you will identify with what you believe in and value.

If you are going to have a curriculum, aka an identity,
It might as well be in alignment with what you truly are –
Love.

There are many curriculums (thought systems) out there.
What matters most is that you and your partner
BOTH Trust your curriculum,
And that you **BOTH** decide to practice it together.

This Manual offers a curriculum.
The curriculum of this Manual is the curriculum of Love.

You are Love.

Therefore this curriculum is both for you,
And about you.

What is the Importance of a Common Curriculum?

It is important to consciously choose a curriculum for your relationship.

Why?

Your curriculum is the ***guidance system*** that will guide you back to Love
When you and your partner forget Love and forget your goal.
And forget, you will.

It is important to Trust your goal and Trust your curriculum more than you
Trust your own thoughts and feelings at any given moment,
Unless those thoughts and feelings are rooted in Love.

What happens if you DO NOT decide to set a common Goal And follow a Common Curriculum?

Since you have both been programmed since birth,
If you do not consciously decide to set a Goal,
You will unconsciously set a goal.

This is called your "default" setting.
And guess what that default setting is?
"The program".

We will discuss the program in more detail later.
For now, the only thing to remember is this:

No good has ever come to anyone from listening to the program. Ever.

And guess what?

The program has a complete curriculum too!
So if you do not consciously choose a curriculum,
Guess what curriculum you will be following by default?
That's right...
The program's curriculum.

And guess what comes from following the program's curriculum?

No good.

WHAT IS A RELATION*SHIP*?
A Vehicle

FriendSHIP
CompanionSHIP
PartnerSHIP

A relationship is a vehicle.
Just like a ship is a vehicle.

All relationships are vehicles.

Relationship = Vehicle
Goal = Destination
Curriculum = Map/GPS

What is the purpose of a vehicle?

The purpose of a vehicle is to transport you somewhere.
You use a vehicle to get to your destination faster and safer
Than you would have without it.

What is the first thing you need to ask before you get into
A vehicle with someone?

"Where are we going?"

Asking this question is important,
Because this is ***Setting the Goal***.
You are discussing and deciding the destination of your journey ***together***.

What happens if you get in a relationship vehicle without a destination?

You will travel around in circles and find yourself in places
You do not want to be in.

What happens if you don't know how to get to your destination?

You will get lost at sea.

How do you get to your destination without getting lost?

Use a map or GPS system.

In relationship terms,
This is called a **CURRICULUM.**

Why have a curriculum?

You can have a common goal (destination) for your relationship,
But how does it serve you if you don't know how to get there?

The curriculum is your map, and your guidance system (GPS).

What happens if you don't know how to operate the vehicle?

You will crash, and you will hurt yourself.
Also known as a **"relation*SHIP WRECK*"**

What causes relationship wrecks?
Listening to the program causes you to have relationship wrecks.
We will cover exactly how the program operates later.
We will expose how its GPS (misguidance system)
Always results in wrecks.

Partnership
Your relationship is a partnership,
Which means you and your partner must operate
Your relationship vehicle together.

Who decides what the Goal and Purpose of your relationship will be?
You and your partner discuss and decide on what the Goal and Purpose
Of your relationship will be.

Who decides what the curriculum of your relationship will be?
You and your partner decide to join on a Common Curriculum.

Just remember:
It is important that the curriculum you decide on
Does NOT come from you or your partner.
Why?

You need a curriculum that is objective, and based on Universal Truth.

What is Universal Truth?

Again, Universal Truth is what is True for everyone, all the time.

As stated before,
A relationship needs these two things in order to be successful:

1. **A Common Goal**
2. **A Common Curriculum**

Without these things,
Your relationSHIP will sink.

Later, you will be shown how to use your internal compass (your feelings)
To know for sure whether or not your relationship vehicle
Is heading in the right direction.

For now,
You and your partner need to *Set the Goal,*
And decide upon a curriculum for your relationship.

Hint:
If you don't already have a curriculum,
You don't have to look far,
This Manual is a curriculum.

Love's Curriculum

Your Relationship is Your Sanctuary
Just Be

What is a Sanctuary?
A Sanctuary is a Holy place.
A Sanctuary is a Loving place.
A Sanctuary is a place you go to remember
Something bigger than yourself.
A sanctuary is a place where you can go and *just BE.*

Be you
Be Free
Be Appreciated
Be Loved
Just for showing up

Love wants your relationship to be a Sanctuary for you and your partner.
If you set the goal and decide on a Common Curriculum,
Your relationship can be all of that and more.

If you do not set the goal and decide on a curriculum,
You will fall into the program's version of what a relationship is:
A prison, a dungeon, an insane asylum, and more.

So...
Do you want Healing in your relationship?
Do you want Peace in your relationship?
Do you want Fun in your relationship?
Do you want Total Fulfillment in your relationship?
Do you want Trust in your relationship?

If so,
Let's get on with setting the goal NOW –

Shall we?

Goal=Purpose (handwritten)

CHAPTER 2
SETTING THE GOAL
What is the Purpose?

<u>THIS IS THE MOST IMPORTANT THING YOU WILL DO</u>
This is the foundation on which this entire Manual is based.

Pay close attention

The Truth is, most partners spend more time and energy
Discussing what's for dinner -
Than discussing why they are even in a relationship with each other.

Just as any partnership or joint venture has a common Goal
And a Mission Statement,
Your relationship should also have a Goal and a Mission Statement.

What is the Goal and Mission Statement?

The Goal is the content.
The Mission Statement is the form.

The Goal is the Purpose of your relationship.
The Mission Statement is the *ways* in which you both join
To support your Goal.

There is another term you've probably heard used in
Relationships referring to the Goal and Mission Statement -
This term is *"vows"*.

What does the program want?

The program wants you to enter into and stay in a relationship
WITHOUT discussing and defining a Goal and Purpose
For your relationship.

What happens when you follow the program?

At best,
Failure to set the Goal results in a relationship that is
Aimless, shiftless, and totally unfulfilling.

At worst, failure to set the Goal results in
Pain, heartache, frustration, and separation.

How do you avoid all that?

Let's start with the Goal.

How Do You set the Goal in Your Relationship?

Have A Conversation

Your Goal is your Purpose.
A Purpose gives your relationship meaning.
It is never too early or too late to decide what
The Purpose of your relationship will be.
It is never too late for you and your partner to commit to that Purpose.

What does it mean to decide on the Purpose?

The Purpose is the content of your relationship.
It is the foundation that everything you do and say will stem from.
The Purpose can be very general, and most importantly:
The Purpose does not change.

Deciding on the Purpose of your relationship is
The most important thing you will do.

Assignment

Have a conversation about your Goal and Purpose
Write down your Goal and Purpose together

Why?
Talking about things is good.
Writing things down makes them real.

Here's an exercise for you and your partner to apply **right now.**

Instructions:

1) Write the Purpose of your relationship down together

Use your dedicated notebook for your relationship and at the top write:
"Our Purpose"
Use the following questions to guide your conversation,
And write down everything that you agree on:

What is the Purpose of our relationship?
What is our relationship for?
What are the reason(s) we are together?
What do we want to come from our relationship?

Next step:

2) Write down your Mission Statement

What is your Mission Statement?

The Goal and Purpose are the CONTENT of your relationship.
The Mission Statement is the FORM your relationship will take.

Remember, the content doesn't change,
But the form *can* and *will* change.
As soon as you decide what your Goal and Purpose are,
Discuss how you would like to express and support that Goal
In your relationship together.

Write your Mission Statement down on a new page, and title it:

"Our Mission Statement"

Use the following questions to guide your conversation:

To fulfill our Goal, what guidelines will we follow?
What curriculum will we use?
How will we express our Goal together?
What are some things we will do to express our Goal?
What will we NOT do to express our Goal?

Example

<u>Setting the Goal for our Relationship</u>
Our Purpose

The Purpose of our relationship is to Love each other.
Our Goal is to give and receive only Love.
We will Love and care about each other.
We will Communicate Honestly, Openly, Fully, and Lovingly.
We will Fully support each other.
We will have Fun, and enjoy our relationship.
We will learn and grow together.

<u>Our Mission Statement</u>
We will express Love to each other by:

Communicating: Sharing only Loving thoughts.
We will each take responsibility for our feelings and our experiences.
We will not attack each other in any way for any reason.
We join only in Love, Play, Fun, Caring,
And Full Acceptance of each other.
We choose NOT to argue.
We will express Appreciation for each other as often as possible.
We will read books and take classes together that
Support our growth and development.
When we feel upset or disturbed, we will not use our feelings as our guide.
We will use Love as our guide.
We will tell the Truth about how we're feeling,
And express Love to each other.
We will use the Manual:
"Love is NOT a Game" as our curriculum,
And follow what it says for us to do.
We will NOT listen to the program or fear when it comes up.
We will travel and take trips together.
...To be continued

If you are sincere, recite your Goal and Mission Statement
To each other every week.
If you're really sincere, recite it each and every day.

WHAT IS SETTING THE GOAL NOT?
About Time

Setting the Goal and Purpose for your relationship is NOT a game.
Therefore, it does not deal with a timeframe.
Only games operate on timeframes.

It is important to understand that the Goal and Purpose of your relationship
Have **ABSOLUTELY NOTHING** to do with time or timeframes.
Why?

Because it will not work.
You cannot control the future.
You do not know what form the future will take for your relationship.
You *can* decide what you will dedicate your relationship to at ALL times.

Here is an example of how **NOT** to set the Goal:

"We will get married in 2 years."
"We will do a 10-day fast together."
"We will move in with each other by _____ date."
"We will eat out every Tuesday night."

Those are not Goals.
Those are *plans*.
Plans are your attempt to control the unknown.
STOP.
Just Stop.
Plans do not establish a Purpose or give your relationship meaning.
A Goal and Purpose give your relationship meaning.
And your Goal and Purpose should be based on the content of Love.

Reminders
Have fun!

Enjoy this experience together!
If you're not having fun, you're not meeting your Goal.

This is a conversation.
Have this conversation.

Discuss the Goal and Purpose of your relationship.

Write it down.
Discuss the Mission of your relationship.
Write it down.
Explore the possibilities together.
Be unattached to any specific outcome.

Remember, the Goal does not change.
The Goal is simple.
It should be short and to the point.
You should be able to remember and recite your Goal to each other easily.

The Mission Statement represents the expression of the Goal in form.
Meaning *how* you decide to Love each other.

The Mission Statement is a fluid, living creation.
It should always develop,
Grow, change, and be added to.
Play around with your Mission Statement.

In Conclusion:
These are the guidelines you develop and agree on with each other about
How you will operate your relationship vehicle.
You are deciding and reminding yourself about the *direction*
You want to travel in, and the direction you don't want to travel in.
You are discussing what you want to experience together.

Don't get stuck doing something if you no longer have Peace doing it.
Play with the variety life has to offer and don't limit yourself.

Once again,
Setting the Goal in your relationship is
The most important thing you will do.

Now that you know how…

Do it!

PART 2
THE TWO CURRICULUMS

LOVE VS
THE PROGRAM

What is Part 2 of this Manual about?

In this part of the Manual,
We will explore the thought system of Love
And the thought system of the program.

We will explain the core principles of Love,
And we will expose the core principles of the program.

What is the purpose of this part of the Manual?

The Purpose of this Part of the Manual is to
Bring clarity to some of the following questions:

- *What is Love really?*
- *What is Love really NOT?*
- *What is the program?*
- *How does Love think?*
- *How does the program think?*
- *What are emotions and feelings?*
- *What is form and content?*
- *What are the two guidance systems?*
- *How do you make decisions?*
- *What is True Freedom?*

Aren't these some great questions?

Let's explore some answers!

CHAPTER 3
THE TWO THOUGHT SYSTEMS
Love or the Program

In this chapter we will be covering the two thought systems:

1. **Love's thought system**
2. **The program's thought system**

A Thought System is a Curriculum.

We will cover the core principles of each thought system.
We will cover what they teach you about yourself,
And what they teach you about your relationship.

You will learn how Love *thinks,*
And how the program *thinks.*
You will learn the lessons of Love,
And the lessons of the program.

You will learn how to identify Love's guidance in your relationship,
And also how to protect yourself from the program's misguidance.

Let's begin.

THE TWO TEACHERS
Guidance systems

Each thought system comes with a teacher.

What is a teacher?
A teacher is a guide.

What does a teacher do?
A teacher offers you guidance (or misguidance).

Your teacher tells you what to do.
Also,
Your teacher tells you how to think, and how to see things.

You are always listening to a teacher.

You have only two teachers.

One teacher is Love.
The other teacher is the program (fear).

What are these teachers teaching you about relationships?
Both of these teachers are teaching you about:
"What you are, and what your partner is to you."

When your relationship is Healthy, meaning Loving,
You do not need help or advice about what to do,
Because Love is Guiding you.

What happens is,
Eventually your programming (fear) will kick in
And try to sabotage your relationship if you listen to it.

Our goal is to learn the difference between the guidance of Love,
And the guidance of fear - which is your insane programming.
In the beginning, it is difficult to differentiate between them,
Why?
Because they sound the same.
The only way to tell the difference between them,
Is the CONTENT of what they're saying.

The content of Love, which is your True guidance,
Is always Healing, Relaxed, and puts no pressure on you about anything.

The content of fear, which is your insane programming,
Is always distressing, difficult,
And puts enormous strain on you about everything.

Each teacher offers a complete thought system.

What is the content of Love's thought system?

Truth, Happiness, Peace, Appreciation,
Innocence, Communication, Fun, Joining.

What is the content of the program's thought system?

The content of the program's thought system is:

Fear, lies, dishonesty, guilt, jealousy, pain, separation.
As you can tell,
These thought systems are diametrically opposed in every possible way.
*They are opposed in **direction,***
*They are opposed in **process,***
*And they are opposed in **result.***

What are Guidance Systems?

When you choose either thought system,
You are activating that *guidance system.*
The guide you choose will give you guidance in accordance
With their thought system, which is their curriculum.

The curriculum of Love is
Peace, and Total Fulfillment
For everyone involved.

The curriculum of the program is
Fear, guilt, attack and pain
For everyone involved.

Are you ready to totally embrace the curriculum of Love?

TRUTH PRINCIPLE
You Will Either Be Host to Love
Or Hostage to the program

There are no in-betweens and no grey areas.

There are only 2 thought systems.

Love is in alignment with your nature.
The program is hazardous to your nature.

When you follow Love - your relationship will be Healthy.
When you follow the program - you will become sick,
And your relationship will become sick.

In the next section, we will discuss the importance of
Developing your immune system against the program.
With immunity, your relationship will not suffer from its sickening effects.

Immune System

Relationship Immunity

In order to remain Healthy,
You have to develop your immune system.

What is the purpose of an immune system?
The purpose of an immune system is to protect you
From things that would make you sick.

In this case,
It is the thought system of the program that would
Make you and your relationship sick.

How does an immune system work?

An immune system can only work if it can
Identify the threat.

If it cannot identify the threat,
It cannot protect you.

Your immune system has been compromised.

Why?

Because the program confuses you about fear and Love.

In order to develop immunity to the program,
You must learn its thought system.
You must learn the principles under which it operates.
You must learn its goal.

When you learn everything about the program,
You will be able to identify it in ALL of its many forms.
Why?

So you can choose *against* it.
When you can identify it *every time,*
You can choose *against* it *every time.*

When you choose against the program (fear),
The result is Love.

DECISION TIME!
Call To Action

Understand that you cannot serve two masters at the same time.
In other words…
You cannot follow two guides that are leading you in opposite directions.

It's time to make a decision.
It's time to take a stand.
Together.

When?

Right NOW

Decide:
Will you take a stand for Love?

*Will you decide that you will accept Love as your **only** Guide?*

*Will you decide that you will learn everything about the program,
Only so you can identify it and reject it when it presents itself?*

*Will you decide that you are willing to follow the curriculum of Love,
And abandon the curriculum of the program?*

*Will you and your partner decide that you are BOTH willing to join
In following ONLY the curriculum of Love from now on?*

*Will you decide to claim your True Inheritance,
Which is Happiness and total fulfillment in your life and relationships?*

If so, please continue.

CHAPTER 4
THE POWER OF DECISION
It's Your Choice

There is only ONE area in your life where you have
Absolute power and authority.

What area is that?

It is in the power of your decision.

Your absolute greatest power is in how you will decide to see things.

How will you decide to perceive right now?

Remember, you are Free.
You are Free to choose how you will see things,
And there are only two ways to see things:

With Love or with fear.

The most important thing you will learn is that Love is a decision.
Fear is also a decision.
You are either consciously choosing to Love,
Or choosing not to Love.

No one wants to choose for fear,
And no one would consciously choose to be afraid.
But remember, everyone is programmed.

So why do I often experience feelings of fear?

Good question.
It happens involuntarily. In other words: **by default.**
Your mind will always return to its default setting when you are not
Actively directing it.

What is your mind's default setting?

Your mind's default setting is fear.
This is not its natural state. This is the result of years of programming.
So programmatic (insane) thinking becomes automatic.

What you are doing now is unlearning and deprogramming that fear,

With the goal for your default thinking to be Loving thoughts.

How do you do this?

Simple.
Decide to **Set the Goal** for Love all the time.

IMPORTANT!

When you do not make a **CONSCIOUS** and **UNDIVIDED DECISION**
To express (give and receive) Love,
You ARE choosing fear by default.
You are choosing the program.

How does that feel?

Fear feels like:
Guilt, distress, drama, judgment, attack, conflict,
Emotional pain, separation, etc.

DECIDE TO TAKE BACK CONTROL OF YOUR MIND!

You can no longer afford to be mentally passive and allow
Your mind and your relationship to run on cruise control.
Because who set the cruise control (default setting)
In your mind and about your relationship?
That's right.

THE PROGRAM

UNIVERSAL PRINCIPLE
Indecisiveness ALWAYS Leads to fear

The question is:

How do you make decisions?

You've learned that there are only two guides from which to decide with.
Love or the program (fear).

So how do you recognize them?
Each guide (or teacher) has rules for making decisions.

It is important you are familiar with these rules.
Why?
So you will always know how to identify what guide you're listening to.

RULES FOR DECISION

PROGRAM DECISIONS	LOVE DECISIONS
Difficulty *It will be difficult for you to do*	*Ease* *It will be easy for you to do*
Unwillingness and Resistance *You don't want to do it*	*Willingness* *You want to do it*
Takes Time *You can't do it now* *Results are in the future*	*Takes No Time* *You can do it right now* *You can experience results right now*
Attached to a Specific Outcome *Expectations*	*Unattached to a Specific Outcome* *Enjoying the experience*

What does this mean?

Let's take a deeper look...

Difficulty vs Ease
When the program guides you to do something,
It's always something that is difficult for you to do.
Love would only guide you to do what's *easy and effortless* for you to do.

Unwillingness and Resistance vs Willingness
The program always wants you to do things that you just *don't want to do.*
Which means you are sacrificing your Peace by doing it.

Love always wants you to do *what you WANT to do.*
You have **Willingness** to do it.

If you are Willing and you want to do something,
It will be easy for you.

Time vs No Time
The program is bound by time.
It believes you are also bound by time.
So it tells you that you can't have what you want right now,
And you can't do what you want right now.
You have to wait to have results.

Love Operates NOW
Love teaches you there is always one thing you can do right now.
And what can you always do right now?
You can make decisions right now.
You can use your power of decision, right now,
And you can decide that you want to see things with Love.

Attached to a Specific Outcome
vs
Unattached to a Specific Outcome
To be attached to a specific outcome is a game.
Only the program is concerned with *"winning"*.
Love knows for certain that there will be a Happy outcome
To all things in your relationship.
Therefore Love is not attached to the *form* the outcome will take.

LOVE PRINCIPLE
It's Only OK if it's OK Either Way

If you remember this one principle when doing anything with your partner,
It will save you both a lot of time.

Being attached to specific outcomes causes strain
Because it comes from expectations.
Expectations put you and your partner under enormous pressure.
What kind of pressure?

Enormous Pressure:
To perform
To show up
To have a certain experience together
To be a certain way
To respond a certain way

Love doesn't involve strain.

Love doesn't involve expectations on any level.

Love doesn't involve pressure of any kind.

Which is why, with Love:

It's only ok, if it's ok either way.

For Example:
When is the best time to do something together?
When it's ok if you don't do it right now.

When is the best time to give your partner a gift?
When they aren't expecting one.
Which means it's ok if you don't give them a gift.

When is the best time to spend time together?
When it's ok if you don't at this time.

Decide:
***Decide you will be totally committed to the experience you are having,
And you will be totally unattached to a specific outcome.***

This is the proper use of your Power.
This is how you decide to let Love lead the way in your relationship.

CHAPTER 5

Clarifying Love

In this chapter we will take a look at what Love is,
And what Love is not.

We will explore the curriculum (thought system) of Love,
And how it operates.

LOVE IS:

Love

*Love just **IS**.*
Love is Love.
Love cannot be defined or explained in words.
Love cannot be understood in words,
Because words are limiting.

Love is Everything.
Love is what you are.
Love is what Created you.
Love is an experience.

The goal of this Manual is for you and your partner to have
The experience of Love together.

LOVE IS: NOT

What is Love NOT?

While we are discussing what Love is,
Let's take a look at what Love is NOT.

Love IS NOT:
- **Love is not a feeling**
  - ○ Although Love can be felt
- **Love is not form**
  - ○ Although Love can take any form

- **Love is not actions**
  - o   Although Love can inspire any action
- **Love is not any specific thing**
  - o   Although anything can be used in the service of Love

The curriculum of Love is the thought system of Love.
You must learn the thought system of Love,
And the thought system of fear.

Although Love cannot be understood, it can be expressed.
Although Love is not a feeling, it can be felt.
You will learn to use your feelings to indicate that you
Are in alignment with Love or out of alignment with Love.
We will cover emotions and feelings in another chapter.

Let's take another look at this idea of Love in the following table:

LOVE IS NOT	LOVE IS
Form	*Content*
Feelings	*Experienced as feelings*
Actions	*The inspiration behind actions*
Things	*Able to use anything to serve its purpose*
A Relationship	*Experienced in a Loving relationship*
A Partner	*Experienced with a Partner*

LOVE IS: YOU

You are Love

Did you create yourself?
No.

What created you?

You were Created by Love.

What are you NOT?
You are not your body. You have a body.
You are not your mind. You have a mind.
You are not your thoughts. You have thoughts.
You are not your feelings. You have feelings.
So what are you?

You are Love.

Your True Self is Love.

This is a Manual about Love.
Which means this is a Manual about You.

Later on we will cover how you express Love in your relationship.
Right now just realize this simple and profound Truth.

You are Love.

LOVE IS: CONTENT
Not Form

The expressions of Love are many, including and not limited to:
*Peace, Appreciation, Honesty, Communication, Trust, Gratitude, Respect,
Care, Freedom, etc.*

When Love is flowing through you and your partner in your relationship,
You will experience *Peace, Appreciation, Honesty, Communication,
Trust, Gratitude, Respect, Care, Freedom, etc.*

LOVE IS: BEYOND TIME AND SPACE
Love operates NOW

Love transcends time and space.
How?

Do you have Loved ones who are not in the same space as you right now?
They may be in the next room, they may be thousands of miles away.

Did you stop Loving them?
No.

Do you still Love them?
Yes.

Do you have Loved ones who have passed on?

Did you stop Loving them?
No.
Do you still Love them?
Yes.

And when do you Love them?
Right now.

Love is not bound by space and time.
Love operates NOW, which is this present moment,
Right now.

The only time to Love is
Right now.

Not yesterday, not tomorrow.
Right now.

When should Love be given?
Right now.

When should Love be received?
Right now.

Now is all you have.
Dedicate your present moment to Love, and let Love lead the way.

Right Now.

LOVE PRINCIPLES
Introducing Love's Core Curriculum

The following is a table of Love's fundamental principles.
These principles govern Love's core curriculum, (or thought system).
More of Love's principles will be covered throughout this Manual.

FUNDAMENTAL PRINCIPLES OF LOVE

PRINCIPLE	WHAT DOES IT MEAN?
Love Cannot be Threatened by Anything	When your relationship is rooted in Love, There is nothing that can threaten your Relationship in any way whatsoever.
Love Has No Levels	**Love is Maximal.** There is no such thing as "More Love" or "less Love" For different people. Love is Maximal.
Love Never Changes	Love stays the same. It never changes with a Person or a circumstance. It is your *awareness* of its presence that can Change and become blocked.
Love is Never Lost	You cannot "lose" Love. You can forget Love. The results of forgetting Love feel like It was never there.
Love is Not Limited	You can Love all the people in your life. You can Love all The books on your bookcase. You cannot exhaust your supply of Love.
Love is Not Painful	Love is never painful in any way. The only time you experience pain is when You are blocking Love from flowing.

Let's take a deeper look…

LOVE IS: ONE

Love is the same for Everyone All the Time

Love is One.
There are no different *"kinds"* of Love.
There are certainly different *expressions* of Love, but only **ONE Love.**

A familiar concept would be *"unconditional Love."*
But this term "unconditional" is redundant and unnecessary.
Love does not need to be qualified by another term.
Love is already unconditional.
Love is.
Saying *"unconditional Love"* is like saying, *"wet water"* or *"hot fire"*.
If it's water, it's going to be wet.
If it's fire, it's going to be hot.
This goes without saying.

Love does not change from person to person, relationship to relationship.
The Love you have for your partner, your friends, your family,
And yourself are all the same Love.

To give you a better idea of what Love is and is not, think about this:

If you have two or more children, which one do you Love more?
If you have two or more Loved ones, which one do you Love more?

The way you *express* Love is the only thing that changes.
All of your relationships will take on a different form,
But all Loving relationships have the same content.

Like water, Love has no set form.
Love can be expressed through any form.
Forms are delivery systems for Love.
We will discuss *form vs. content* later.

For now, focus on the principle:

Love *Is One.*

Love Is: Simple

And Easy

Love is simple.
Love is easy.
Love is effortless.
There is nothing complicated about Love.
There is nothing complicated about a relationship based on Love.

A Loving relationship is the easiest thing in the world to have.

Only the program makes things complicated, complex, and confusing.

The message of this Manual is about Love
Therefore the message of this Manual is simple.

Again,

Love is Simple. Love is Total. Love is One. Love is Unlimited.
There are no kinds of Love.
There is only Love, or the blocking of Love, called fear, or the program.
Love is unconditional.
Love is content and not form.
The content of Love does not change with anyone or anything.
It is either being expressed in the moment, or not.

Love does not change with a person or a circumstance.
Love does not increase or decrease.
Love is always maximal, and Love is always available.
You do not have a choice about how Love operates.
Your choice lies in whether you choose to Love
Or to block Love in the moment.

"To Love, or not to Love...?"

THAT *is the question.*

LOVE IS

Love is
Nothing forced,
Nothing held back.

Love is
Never anxious,
Always Relaxed.

Love is
Only Healing,
Never attack.

Love is
Total Abundance,
Never lacks.

Love is
A way to Extend,
Not contract.

Love is
Truly Helpful,
With every act

Love is

CHAPTER 6
THE PROGRAM
The Reason Why Relationships Fail

In this chapter we will expose the insane thought system of the program.

Why are we looking at the program?

Because the Truth is:
Everyone is programmed.
You have been programmed.
Your partner has been programmed.
Everyone you know has been programmed,
And everyone you don't know has been programmed.

This is good to know,
Because knowing is half the battle.

The question is:
Programmed how?

We will take a look at:

The program's purpose,
How it operates,
Its core principles,
How it plays games with your mind,
And with your heart.

By learning its curriculum, you will learn why relationships fail.
You will also learn what NOT to do in your relationship.

Ready?

Let's begin.

What is the Program?
The Part of Your Mind That Wants You to Destroy Yourself

The program is a thought system.

It is a thought system rooted in *fear.*

What is fear?
Fear is what is experienced when Love is blocked.

When were you programmed?

You have been programmed since birth.
You have been programmed to look upon the world and
Everything and everyone in it with fear.

You were not born with the program,
You were exposed to it.
It is a thought system that was taught to you,
And you learned it.

This fearful programming seeps into your relationships,
And causes emotional pain.

Dis-ease
Temporary Insanity

The program is a thought system based on insanity.
It can be seen as a mental disease.
Why?
Because it causes you mental and emotional dis-ease.
Which means,
When the program is running in your mind -
You are temporarily insane.

What's the first thing you need to know to cure any disease?

HOW TO RECOGNIZE IT
Diagnosis

You cannot cure a disease if you do not know it's there.
You cannot cure a disease if you do not know how to identify it.

After you identify it, you can take the necessary steps to cure it,
And prevent it from making you sick again.

AN INSANE CURRICULUM
A Complete Thought System

The program is a curriculum,
Which means it is a complete thought system.
Unfortunately,
It is a thought system that is diametrically opposed
To Love's thought system in every way.

How do you evaluate a thought system?
You can only evaluate a thought system based on its results.
The results of following the program are consistent.

What are the results of following the program?
The results of following the program are always:

*Guilt, grief, distress, conflict, attack, arguments, anger, hatred,
Disappointment, uncertainty, upset, suspicion, conflict,
Pain, loss and ultimately separation.*

When you experience any of these results
At any point in any relationship –
It is a direct result of following the program's curriculum.

If these are not the results you want:

Don't follow it.

GOAL OF THE PROGRAM
What is the Purpose of the Program?

The purpose of the program is to cause you to forget Love.
When you forget Love, you experience fear.
When you listen to fear, you will hurt yourself.

Therefore, the purpose of the program is:

To cause you to feel separate from Love.
To cause you to hurt yourself.
To cause you pain.

THE PROGRAM IS NOT REAL
Blocked Love

It is important to remember that fear is not real,
Meaning the program is not real.
Only Love is real.
So when you experience fear,
You are experiencing what it feels like to block Love.

Sometimes this experience is called:

- Anger
- Loss
- Guilt
- Insanity
- Jealousy
- Insecurity
- Sadness
- Emotional pain

It's all the same.
It's all a game.

How do you get rid of the program?

The experience of fear is like darkness. It has no source.
You cannot get rid of darkness by attacking it,
Analyzing it, or arguing with it.
The only way to dispel darkness is with light -
Meaning unblocking Love.

Love is always present,
Love is like the sun.
Fear is like a cloud that blocks the sun,
So it seems dark.

To have the sunlight, you don't have to get the sun to shine brighter -
You have to remove the block (the clouds).

For Example:
If it's sunny outside and it's dark inside,
It's because the blinds are blocking out the light.
You do not have to wish for more sun.

What do you have to do?

Remove the blinds.

PROGRAM PRINCIPLES
Introducing the Program's Core Curriculum of Insanity

The following is a table of the program's fundamental principles of fear.
These principles govern the program's core curriculum (thought system).
These principles are based on absolute insanity.

PROGRAM PRINCIPLE	WHAT IT MEANS
Love can be Threatened by Anything	The program does not know what Love is. The program is afraid of everything. It believes that absolutely anything can threaten Your Love and your relationship.
There are Levels to Love	The program thinks Love can be measured. It tells you there is more Love at times, And less Love at other times. More Love for some, less Love for others – *Sometimes.*
There are Different Kinds of Love	The program believes there are different kinds Of Love for different forms of relationships.
Love is Special	The program believes Love can be reserved For a few select people and relationships. Love is not for everyone.

Love is Limited	The program believes there is only so much Love to go around. So you should be very Selective about who you give your Love to.
Seek and Do NOT Find	The program wants you to seek for Love where It is NOT located. Meaning outside of you. In another person, in another relationship.
Love and fear are the Same. You can have Love And fear at the Same Time	The program thinks that Love and attack are the same. It teaches you that it is possible to Love Someone and hate them at the same time.
Conflict is Good	In a programmatic relationship, The more conflict you have - the better. Conflict and arguments mean you care.
You are Your Body	The program believes you are your body and Your partner is their body. Therefore it becomes *extremely* important what You do and don't do with your body.
Your Feelings Should Guide You	The program wants your relationship to be Unstable and in constant conflict. So it tells you that you should say and do Things based *entirely* on how you *feel* at any Given moment.
Get and Keep	The program would enter a relationship only To get something and keep it for itself.
Love is Form	The program believes Love is represented by Material things, deeds, forms, etc.
Love is Painful	The program thinks Love is painful because it Thinks Love and fear are the same. Only fear brings about emotional pain.

That's enough of that for now.

What is going on here?

In a word,
CONFUSION.

Confusion is very important to the program.
Remember, the program wants to control you.
And when it can confuse you, it can control you.
Why?
Because when you're confused,
What will you do?
You will look for guidance.
And the program WILL offer you guidance.
But it will offer you its fearful misguidance,
Which is designed to serve its fearful purpose.
Its purpose is for you to forget Love.
Don't be fooled.

Let's take a deeper look at some of the program's fearful principles.

PROGRAM PRINCIPLE
Your Love Can be Threatened by Anything

According to the program,
Your relationship can be threatened by just about anything -

*A thought, a feeling, an action, a phone call, a text,
Another person, another relationship, etc.*
This is an illusion.

Remember,
True Love cannot be threatened by anything.

PROGRAM PRINCIPLE
There are Different Kinds of Love

The program teaches you that there are different kinds of Love.

For example:

There's a kind of Love you have for your family,
A kind you have for your partner or Lover,
A kind you have for your friends,
A kind you have for your colleagues, your work, your passion in life, etc.

There are no *kinds* of Love.
Love is always One.

PROGRAM PRINCIPLE
Love Can Be Painful

The program confuses you further by telling you that
Love is joyous at times and painful at times.
That Love has the capacity to hurt and to Heal.
That you have to Love yourself, but Love is sacrifice and selflessness.

This is insanity of the highest order.
Love is Healing.
Period.

PROGRAM PRINCIPLE
You Can Have Love and Fear at the Same Time

This is where the program further continues its
Campaign of conflict, contradiction and confusion about Love.

The program teaches you that it is possible to
Love and hate at the same time.
It teaches you that it is possible to have Love and fear at the same time.
It teaches you that it is possible to Love someone
And be afraid of them at the same time.

No.

You cannot have light and darkness at the same time.
You cannot have Love and fear at the same time.
You have all of one or all of the other - at any time.

Period.

PROGRAM PRINCIPLE
There are Levels to Love

The program teaches you that it is possible to Love one person
More than another.
It teaches you that it is possible to care about someone
More than someone else.

This is impossible.

Love is One.
Love is the same for everyone.

PROGRAM PRINCIPLE
Seek and Do NOT find

To keep you under its control,
The program wants you to seek for Love where it is not.
What better way to get someone to keep coming back to you for guidance
Than to keep them lost?

Where is Love NOT?

Love is not outside of you.

The program teaches you to seek for Love where it is not:

- In another person
- In a relationship
- In sex
- In material things
- In what you do
- In what others do

Love is within.

WHY DON'T PROGRAMMATIC RELATIONSHIPS WORK?

How the program tries To Fool You

As you know, the program is a complete thought system.

Which means:
For every question you have about your relationship,
The program has an answer for you.
For every problem that comes up in your relationship,
The program has a solution for you.

The real problem is -
It only gives *programmatic* solutions,
Which do not Heal, but only cover the wound, temporarily.

Even if you find temporary relief from listening to the program,

What happens?

The wound gets reopened, and you suffer again.

Maybe in a different form...
Maybe at a different time...
Maybe in a different relationship...

But suffer you will.
Because,
Make no mistake about it...

The program hates you.

Why?
Because the program hates Love.

Why?

The program is afraid of Love

Why?

Because Love dispels the program,
And Heals ALL of its hurtful effects.

Love is about joining.
The program is about separation.

Love is about Healing.
The program is about hurting.

So,
The very thing that will keep your relationship whole and Happy –
Would destroy the program.

The good news is:
YOU don't have to focus on *"destroying"* the program.
It's not real anyway.
It's an illusion.

Focus on Love.
Focus on being Happy.

When you focus on Love,
Your Loving experience will show you that the program
Never existed in the first place –
And you will no longer react with fear,
To what was never there.

THE PROGRAM IS A GAME

Hardcore Gamer

The program is a hardcore gamer. It plays games.
It plays games all the time.
Playing games is all it does, all it ever did, and all it ever will do.
Do not expect it to change, because it won't.
The program itself is a game.

What is its end game?
The program's only end game is to ruin your relationship,
And cause pain and separation from Love.

In short:
To waste your time.

How do you beat it at its game?

You cannot change the program.
All you can do is stop following it.

Trying to beat the program at its game,
Is like trying to escape from a prison
With a map handed to you by a prison guard.

Will that map lead you to Freedom?

No!

That is what happens when you ask the program for guidance.

Remember,
The program has an answer for EVERY question you could possibly have,
But all of its answers serve **its** purpose.

What's its purpose?

To confuse you.
To separate you.
To get you to hurt yourself.

Nothing it says can be Trusted.

If you're going to escape its prison (thought system),
You're going to need a map that comes from *beyond* the prison.

Love's map.

Why play the program's game?
You can't win.

Who made the rules?
It made the rules, not you.

So,
How do you win the game?

The only way to win is not to play.

IF THE PROGRAM WERE A PERSON
What Kind of Crazy Person is This?

We've reviewed many of the program's insane ideas
About Love in this chapter.

You have to ask yourself:
How can one thing (Love) be so many things at the same time?
How can it have so many conflicting qualities and still be True?

Have you ever wondered?
"If the program were a person, what kind of person would it be?"

The program would be a person walking around calling itself "Love",
But giving Love a bad name.

If the program were a person applying for a job,
Their application would be rejected.

Why?

Because no one would be able to figure out just who this person is
Or what they actually do.

How can they have so many different faces?

They claim that they mean well,
But they do so many conflicting things that cause
Confusion, chaos, and conflict.

How can they be helpful at times and hurtful at times?

This profound confusion about Love is an example of the program
Succeeding at its goal.

Its goal being to cause confusion, separation, and pain.
Its goal being to cause you to *distrust* Love.

What better way to get you to distrust someone or something
Than to make them appear to be unreliable, inconsistent, and dishonest?

How could you Trust something or someone who is
Supposed to be helping you,
But at the same time they are hurting you?

How could you Trust someone who you know to be a certain way,
Yet in another relationship, you wouldn't even recognize them?

If the program's version of Love were a person,
You would conclude that this person is quite insane.
By any standards they would be insane.

Would you Trust someone like that?

Of course not!

So then –

Why would you Trust anything the program teaches you?

BEWARE THE PROGRAM
It's Infectious

Do not put the program in charge of your relationship.

The program's thought system is the poison of all relationships.

And do not think that just because you know about the program

That your relationship cannot be infected by it.

Your relationship is not special and the program gives no special favors.

You have not as yet built up your immunity to the program.

No relationship can survive the insanity of the program

Without getting sick, becoming dysfunctional and dying.

Recognize the program in ALL its forms,

And decide to go the other way –

Together.

CHAPTER 7
EMOTIONS AND FEELINGS
You Are An Emotional-Feeling Being

In this chapter we will be exploring the Truth about emotions and feelings.
The goal of this chapter is to give you a *simple* understanding
About your emotions and feelings.

We will be exploring these questions:

What are emotions?
What are feelings?
How do they function?
What do they mean?
What do they look like when they are aligned with Love?
What do they look like when they are not aligned with Love?
How can they be used to serve your relationship?

Interesting questions right?

Let's explore!

THE TWO EMOTIONS
Love and Fear

You are an emotional being.
As an emotional being,
You are only ever experiencing one of two emotions at any time.
What are the two emotions?
Love and fear.

Love *is what you are.*
Fear *is what you have learned.*
Love is real.
Fear is not real.
Love is of you.
Fear is of the program.
Love is everything.
Fear is nothing.

Fear is the absence of Love
Just as darkness is the absence of light.

We will be looking at the common results
And *expressions* of these two emotions:
Love and fear.

What about feelings?

You have only two *emotions*,
And there are *many, many* ways of expressing them.
The expressions of these emotions are what are commonly called
Your feelings.

The table below is a list of common expressions and feelings.
On one side are the expressions and feelings that come from Love,
On the other side are the expressions and feelings that come from fear.
Remember, fear is nothing.
Fear is the result of blocking Love.

UNIVERSAL EXPRESSIONS OF LOVE AND FEAR

EXPRESSIONS OF FEAR	EXPRESSIONS OF LOVE
Misery	*Joy*
Sadness	*Happiness*
Boredom	*Fun, Play*
Guilt	*Innocence*
Distrust, Suspicion	*Trust*
Lies, Illusions	*Truth*
Resistance	*Willingness*
Analysis, Judgment, Processing	*Acceptance*
Holding grievances	*Forgiveness*
Separation	*Joining*
Seriousness	*Sincerity*

Dishonesty	Honesty
Arguing	Communication
Conflict	Peace
Closed	Openness
Confusion	Clarity
Insanity	Sanity
Denial, Attack, Defense	Allowance
Guarded, Shielded	Vulnerability
Blocking	Surrender
Hurt, pain	Healing
Apathy	Empathy
Impatience	Patience
Disturbed	Calm
Doubt	Certainty
Taking for granted, Ungrateful	Appreciation, Gratitude
Exclusive	Inclusive
Insecurity, Jealousy	Secure
Loss	Gain
Hoarding	Sharing
Scarcity	Abundance
Imprisonment	Freedom
Apprehension, Uncertainty	Confidence, Conviction
Disbelief	Belief
Weakness	Strength

ALL OR NOTHING
Universal Principles

Remember Universal Principles?
Well guess what?

Love is a Universal Principle.
Fear is also a Universal Principle.

What does this mean?

This means that all of the expressions of Love contain
The FULL CONTENT of Love.

All of the expressions of fear contain
The FULL CONTENT of fear.

The content of Love or fear can be expressed in ANY form whatsoever.

You cannot have *"a little bit"* of Love and *"a little bit"* of fear.
The two cannot mix.
You either have ALL of one,
Or ALL of the other.
Never neither.
Never both.

In other words...

If you are experiencing ANY expression of Love –
You are experiencing Love.
Period.

If you are experiencing ANY expression of fear,
You are experiencing fear.
Period.

It doesn't matter what you decide to call it.

For a deeper understanding of how simple this idea is –

Let's take a look at the following two tables:

TABLE 1 – EXPRESSIONS

EXPRESSING LOVE OR FEAR	
THIS MEANS	**THAT**
I Trust... *I Appreciate...* *I Join with...* *I am Open to...* *I Accept...* *I Free...* *I Care about...* *I Respect...* *I Support...* *I am Honest...*	*I Love*
I am afraid... *I attack...* *I resist...* *I don't Trust...* *I have conflict with...* *I am closed to...* *I am suspicious of...* *I am jealous...* *I am angry...* *I want to be separate...*	*I Fear*

[TABLE 2 ON NEXT PAGE]

TABLE 2 - FEELINGS

FEELING LOVE OR FEAR	
This Means	*That*
I feel Happy *I feel Excited* *I feel Calm* *I feel Free* *I feel Peace* *I feel Enthusiastic* *I feel Abundant* *I feel Generous* *I feel Good* *I feel Decisive* *I feel Willing*	*I Feel Love* *I Feel Loving*
I feel anxious *I feel distressed* *I feel angry* *I feel confused* *I feel burdened* *I feel indecisive* *I feel lack* *I feel upset* *I feel attacked* *I feel abandoned* *I feel guilty*	*I Feel Fear* *I Feel Afraid*

A LOOK AT YOUR FEELINGS
You Are Not Your Feelings

Love is not a feeling, although Love can be felt.
How is Love felt?

When you are feeling
Compassionate, Enthusiastic, Happy, Peaceful, Generous
And any of Love's expressions –
You are feeling Love.

When you are feeling
*Upset, annoyed, impatient, angry, hurt, disappointed, jealous, guilty
And any of fear's expressions –*
You are blocking Love.

Love can be felt and expressed through your feelings,
But Love is NOT a feeling.

Why is Love NOT a feeling?

Remember the Principle?
Love does not change.

What do feelings do all the time?
Feelings Change.

Alright now.

WHAT ARE FEELINGS?
Your Internal Experiences

There is no such thing as "negative" feelings or "positive" feelings.
Why?
Because "negative" and "positive" are judgments.
Love does not judge.
To judge is to attack.
Love does not judge the feelings you are having,
And Love does not judge you for having them.

Your feelings are simply internal experiences.

You may like your experiences or you may not like your experiences.
Your experiences do not define or change who you are at your core.
You are Love.

The program wants you to judge yourself.
It wants you to judge yourself based on how you feel,
Especially when you are feeling disturbed.

According to the program:
*When you feel sad, you ARE sad.
When you feel angry, you ARE angry.
When you feel guilty, you ARE guilty.*

82

You're guilty because you've done something wrong,
And you deserve to be punished.

These are lies!

According to Love:
When you feel sad, you are experiencing sadness.
When you feel angry, you are experiencing anger.
When you feel guilty, you are experiencing guilt.
You did nothing wrong, and you do not deserve to be punished.
You deserve to be Loved, regardless of how you feel about yourself.

Remember,
The goal is to remember Love.
Just because you may forget Love temporarily,
That doesn't mean Love has abandoned you.
You ARE Love.
You cannot be separate from Love.
You can forget who you are,
But forgetting who you are does not stop you from BEING who you are.

HOW ARE FEELINGS CREATED?
All Feelings Are Self-Generated

Your feelings come about by how you choose to see things.
There are only two ways to see anyone or anything –
With Love, or without Love, which is fear.

Thinking is seeing.

TRUTH PRINCIPLE
Thoughts Lead to Feelings

When you think about someone or something,
There is *ALWAYS* an emotion attached.

Since there are only two emotions,
Understanding how feelings are created is very simple.

Let's use an equation.

Here is the equation:

> ***Thought + Emotion = Feeling***
>
> *More specifically:*
>
> **Your Thoughts**
> *(What you think)*
> **+**
> **Your Emotional State**
> *(Love or fear)*
> **=**
> **Your Feelings**
> *(How you feel)*

In other words:
What you think about,
With Love or with fear,
Becomes how you feel.

What does this mean?

<u>TRUTH PRINCIPLE</u>
You Have No Neutral Thoughts

Love and fear are NOT neutral states.
You are ALWAYS in one of those states.
Whatever you think about in a state of Love will result in Loving feelings:
Joy, Happiness, Peace, Acceptance, Contentment, etc.

Whatever you think about from a state of fear
Will result in unloving feelings (fear):
Guilt, upset, anger, sadness, jealousy, separation, etc.

For example:

If you think about your partner from a state of anxiety (fear),
You will cause yourself to feel worried (fear).

If you think about your partner from a state of Trust (Love),
You will allow yourself to feel Peace (Love)

The big question:

How do I change the way I feel when I'm feeling upset (fear)?

When you find yourself feeling upset for any reason,
It is ALWAYS because you are listening to the thought system of fear.
The program.
Listening to the program automatically puts you in a state of fear.

Remember,
*There is a way Love thinks,
And there is a way fear thinks.
These are called* **Thought Systems.**

When you decide to think with Love's thought system,
You will naturally experience Loving feelings.

When you think with the program's thought system,
You will experience fearful feelings.

So, once again:
How do you change your feelings???

CHANGE YOUR THINKING

Decide to **STOP.**
Just stop.

Stop what?

Stop listening to the program as your guide.
Choose to listen to Love's guidance.

Do not attack yourself for having upsetting feelings.
They are part of your human experience.
If your feelings aren't coming from Love,
They don't mean anything.
You give them all the meaning they have.

A question for you is:
What meaning will **YOU** *give them?*

Next question:
What should you do about your feelings?

Feel your feelings!
Allow your feelings!
Experience your feelings!
Observe your feelings!

And certainly,
DO NOT JUDGE YOUR FEELINGS!

Your feelings are your internal experiences,
Experience them.

EMOTIONAL PAIN
But Why Though?

Have you ever asked yourself:

Why do I experience emotional pain?

When you experience emotional pain, even for a moment,
In that moment, you are not experiencing Love.

Remember,
Love does not hurt, and Love does not get hurt.
If you Love someone, you never want them to be in pain.
If someone Loves you, they never want you to be in pain.
Simple as that.

The confusion comes when you are in a relationship
With someone you Love,
Something happens,
And in the next moment you feel hurt, upset, betrayed, abandoned, etc.

What is that moment?
That is a moment where you have allowed the program to
Hijack your mind.
That is why you feel pain.
The program teaches you that you are a victim of your fearful feelings.
That is why you feel pain.
The program tells you that your partner is to blame.
That is why you feel pain.

All emotional pain is a result of listening to the program.

You are about to learn how you can use even your unloving feelings
To guide you and your partner back to Love –
By asking one simple question.

USING YOUR FEELINGS CORRECTLY
Your Feelings are Indicators

How does the program teach you to use your feelings?

The program teaches you to use your feelings about your partner as a guide
For how you should treat them and interact with them.
The program teaches you to use your feelings to make final judgments
About your relationship and about your partner in that moment.
And the program teaches you to use that impulsive judgment
To decide if you should extend Love to your partner or not.

According to the program:
If you are feeling Loving feelings towards your partner,
Then your partner is worthy of Love.
If you're not feeling Loving feelings towards your partner,
Then they do not deserve Love.
Nothing could be further from the Truth.

Listening to your unloving feelings will cause you pain
And place unnecessary strain on your relationship.
Listening to your unloving feelings will result in separation,
Which is the program's goal.

What is the correct use of feelings?

There is a way to use both your Loving and unloving feelings
To serve your relationship.

How?

As indicators.

Your feelings will ALWAYS tell you the Truth about this one question:

"What guide are you listening to right now?"

Love or the program?

TRUTH PRINCIPLE
Your Feelings are Indicators of Your State of Mind

How do you identify what guide you're listening to?

Ask yourself this one simple question:

"Do I like how I feel right now?"

If the answer is:
"Yes, I like how I feel right now"

You are listening to Love.
Proceed.

If the answer is:
"No, I do not like how I feel right now"
You are listening to the program.
Do not proceed.

STOP.
Just stop.

You may ask:
"What if the answer is something other than 'yes' or 'no'?
Such as:
'Well...I don't know how I feel right now. I'm confused'"

That's easy.

You're listening to the program.

So STOP.
Just stop.

Love is never unsure, Love is always sure.
Only the program does not know what anything is for.
Only the program is ever doubtful.

Understand,
You are either a TOTAL YES,
Or a TOTAL NO.

Here's a simple rule to remember:

ANYTHING other than a TOTAL YES
Is a TOTAL NO.

Love is always a TOTAL YES.
Then who's a TOTAL NO?

Take a wild guess,
You already know.

MAKE A DECISION
Choose to See it Differently

Here are some simple decisions to make that will bring more Love
And Happiness into your life and relationship instantly.

Decide, right now, that **whenever you are feeling upset:**
(Afraid, suspicious, jealous, guilty, or angry) about your partner...

Decide
"I do not like how I feel right now."

Decide
"I am not seeing my partner with Love."

Decide
"I am listening to the program right now,
And the program is always wrong about everything and everyone."

Decide
"There is another way of seeing my partner."

Decide
"I WANT another way to see my partner."

Decide
"I WANT to be Happy more than I want to be right about this."

Question:
Would you rather be right, or would you rather be Happy?

If you are not Happy,
Why would you want to be right about how you are seeing things?

You are not wrong, you are just listening to the wrong guide.

The program

The program is always wrong about everything and everyone.

Love is always right, and Love is always Happy.

So, you can have both:

You can be right AND Happy by being Loving.

Only you can allow Love, and only you can block Love.
Nothing anyone says or does has the power to hurt you.

Remember your goal.
Your goal is not to seek for Love

Your goal is to remember Love.
Love is a choice.

And Love is NOT a Game

CHAPTER 8

FORM AND CONTENT
You Give Form All the Meaning That It Has For You

Here is a topic that the program uses as a major source of confusion.
Form and content.
We will explore this topic with the goal of making it very clear,
And applicable.

Approach
We will cover what form is, and what content is.
We will cover the principles that govern them.
We will cover how the program sees form, and how Love sees form.
We will cover how any form can be used to serve
The Love in your relationship.

Let's begin.

What is form?
For the purposes of this Manual, form can be defined as:
Everything you can think of.
For example:
Thoughts, words, actions, things, time, space,
And anything that can be threatened.

What is content?
There are only two kinds of content.
Love and fear.

What is the Principle that governs form and content?

TRUTH PRINCIPLE
Love is Content, and Not Form of Any Kind
Fear is Content, and Not Form of Any Kind

How does this work?
Although Love and fear are both content, they can take on any form.

What is the difference between content and form?

Content = *Substance, Essence*
Form = *Delivery System, Vehicle, Channel*

Let's apply this idea to something rather familiar –
A TV for example:

When you watch TV,
What do you watch? The TV, or what's on the TV?
You don't sit and watch a blank television screen.

What do you watch?
You watch the CONTENT on the TV.
It could be a TV show, movie, the news, etc.
The TV is the FORM or *delivery system* for the CONTENT you watch.

To take it further:
The content (TV show) is not limited by the form (TV),
Yet you can watch the same content on any TV.

The form (TV) does not even matter.
You can watch your content on a computer, smartphone, tablet, etc.
Those are all delivery systems.
If your TV breaks, you can get another TV,
Or watch your show somewhere else.

But, if your show was cancelled,
Could you continue watching it on any TV in the world?
No.

So what's more important?
Form or content?

How does this relate to Love and fear?

As stated earlier,
Love and fear are <u>content</u>, and <u>not form</u> of any kind.

What makes this concept simple to understand is that Love and fear
Are the ONLY TWO kinds of content.

Yet the forms you can express them in are limitless.

For example:
You can express Love through
A text, a card, a gift, a relationship, or a marriage.
You can also express fear through
A text, a card, a gift, a relationship, or a marriage.

If this is the case...
It leads us to a very important question.

What do the forms –
(The text, the card, the gift, the relationship, the marriage, etc.)
REALLY MEAN?

Are you ready?

The forms mean ABSOLUTELY NOTHING.

All forms have exactly *zero* meaning in and of themselves.

You might ask...
*Ok, so since Love and fear are the **only two** meanings to give anything,*
Where does anything get its Loving or fearful meaning from?

Guess who?

FROM YOU

FUNDAMENTAL TRUTH PRINCIPLE
Form Means Absolutely Nothing
You give Everything all the Meaning that it has (for you)

What does that mean?

It means that nothing on this earth, including your relationship,
Has any inherent meaning.
The meaning comes from the perceiver - you.

The program would teach this:
Everything has meaning!
A chair has meaning, you sit on it.
Words have meaning! We use them to communicate!
For example,
If you use profane language when talking to someone,
You are insulting them.
If you use kind, formal language, you are respecting them.
Ha!

Guess what?

None of that means anything.

Love teaches this:
Nothing has meaning until you give it meaning.
What determines the meaning?
The Purpose.
The purpose you give something gives it its meaning.
Using the same examples:
If you use a chair to help someone get something from a high shelf,
The chair is being used for the purpose of being truly helpful,
Which is an expression of Love.

If you get angry at someone and throw the chair at them,
The chair is being used for the purpose of attack,
Which is an expression of fear.

Chairs have no inherent meaning. They are not only for sitting,
Chairs are for whatever you want them to be for.

The same goes for words and language.
What do words mean?
Absolutely Nothing.

Profane language and formal language mean absolutely nothing,
Because language means absolutely nothing.

If you use "profane" language with someone who
Loves using profane language to express themselves.
They will be comfortable with it.
If you use the same "profane" language with someone who
Gives it an upsetting meaning,
They will be upset.
If you use the very same "profane" language with someone who doesn't
Even speak your language,
They would be confused,
Because they have no idea what you're saying.

Those are three examples using the same form ("profane" language)
And three totally different responses.

So how could anything you say have a consistent meaning
If it is given a different meaning by each person you say it to?

In conclusion:
If the words don't invoke the same response from everyone,
Every time you use them,
The words are totally meaningless.
You give the words all the meaning they have to you.

Again, this principle is not limited to words. It is a Universal Principle. It covers everything you can possibly think of on the level of form.

That is why everything on the level of form becomes a
Delivery System.
For content.

The content being what?
Love or fear.
There are no in-betweens.

You are either fully expressing Love, or fully expressing fear.

There is no such thing as neutral content.
In any given moment you are fully committed to one or the other
As your teacher and guide.
Only forms are neutral, because they don't mean anything.
They are simply delivery systems for the content.

Just as your TV is the delivery system for your media,
So is your computer, your tablet, and your friend's TV.
Same content, different delivery systems (forms).

Your words can be delivery systems for:
Appreciation, Communication, Honesty and Truth in your relationship.

Or your words can be delivery systems for:
Attack, arguments, guilt, and lies in your relationship.

It's your choice.

PROGRAM PRINCIPLE
Form is most Important and form has Inherent Meaning
If you Aim for the Ideal Form, the Ideal Content will Follow

Nothing could be further from the Truth.

This is insanity.
The program teaches that as long as your relationship follows
A certain script or form –
That means it is a good relationship.

What kind of advice would the program give you on this topic?
The program would give you the following relationship advice:

You have been with this person for a certain amount of time,
It's time to move in together!
Just set the goal to move in together, and your Love will deepen!
If you don't take that step,
Your relationship will have less meaning and will fail!

That advice is horrible.
Don't take it.

What advice would Love give?

Love would say:
What is your goal? Content or form?
Have you set the goal for your relationship yet?
Set the goal to Love and support each other's total Peace of mind.
Setting the goal to move in together will not guarantee total Peace of mind.

Set the goal for Content:
Love, Trust, Peace, Full Appreciation, Communication,
Honesty, Joining and Authenticity.

Focus only on those things,
And don't be attached to the form of the outcome.
Commit totally to your goal.
Love will reveal to you the form your relationship should take at any
And all times to allow that Loving content to flow.

Remember, you are a creator.
You give everything a purpose, and therefore a meaning to you.
As partners in a relationship, you are co-creating your experience together.

Now that you have this knowledge, it's time to put it into use.

ONLY LOVE HAS MEANING
The Goal of Your Relationship is Love

Love is the only meaningful thing in the Universe.
So, if something is done or said without Love,
It does not mean anything.

Everything done in the Spirit of Love is totally meaningful.
Everything done or said in a state of fear is totally meaningless.
It is not even worth being responded to.

CONVERSATION TIME
Have a Conversation Based on These Questions

What have you learned about form and content?

Of the two, which has meaning?

Which is meaningless?

Who gives meaning to everything?

What are the only two kinds of content?

What does the program want you to focus on?
Form or content?

What does Love want you to focus on?
Form or content?

Next will be your assignment.

Assignment

Decide
There are some decisions for you and your partner to make **right now**
For this knowledge to be practical to your relationship.

Ready?

Will you decide right now –
To give the content of Love ALL the meaning
In your Life and your relationship?

Will you decide right now –
To give the content of fear NO meaning whatsoever?

Will you decide right now –
That you want Love above all else?

Will you decide right now –
To see everything on the level of form as a neutral delivery system?

Will you decide right now –
To put every form into the service of Love?

Decide to give and receive only Love from now on.
Because…

If not now,
When?

If not you,
Who?

If not here,
Where?

If not this relationship,
Which relationship?

You have the power of decision.
You can decide to see everything with Love.

Start now.
This is not a game.

CHAPTER 9
LOVE IS FREEDOM
You Are Free

Always do what you want to do
And don't do what you don't want to do
Leave grown folks alone

Love is Freedom
What is the statement of Freedom?

"Do what you want to do,
And don't do what you don't want to do."

This is Freedom.
Applying this idea to your life and relationship
Will save you a lot of time.

We are going to talk about Freedom in this Chapter.
First, let's look at the psychosis of the program:

If the content of Love is Freedom, what is the content of the program?

Imprisonment.

You are Free, which means that everything you do
You do because you WANT to do it.
If you do something you do not FULLY want to do,
You will experience a sense of strain.

Do you ever wonder why you feel hesitant when
Accepting gifts from certain people?
*When someone calls you, why do you feel an **obligation** to call them back?*
Why do you feel you need to call them within a particular timeframe?
Why is there so much resistance here?

The reason you feel resistance is because you are Free,
And these are expressions of imprisonment.
Experiencing strain and imprisonment are the result of
Following the program.
What does the program teach?
The program teaches that everything you do,

You do so that you can GET something in return.
The motivation for doing anything is because you want to
GET something in return for it.
This never works.

IMPRISONMENT IN RELATIONSHIPS
Reciprocity and Expectations
Transactions and Bargains

PROGRAM PRINCIPLE
Have Expectations
Especially Silent Expectations

PROGRAM PRINCIPLE
The Only Reason to do Anything is to
GET Something in Return for Doing it

How does the program imprison?
When the program gives you anything, it expects something in return.
Everything that comes from the program has a *cost* attached to it.
Which means, it tries to place you in debt to it.
When you choose to accept what the program gives you,
You place yourself in debt to it.

How does this work?
Silent Expectations
Again, whenever the program gives, it expects something in return.
It doesn't always *say* that it's expecting anything in return, but it is.
This silent expectation places unbearable strain on you both.

How do you know it's expecting something from you if it doesn't say so?
You know because if you DON'T give it something it wants in return –
It will be disappointed, and it will blame you for how it feels.
This is debt and imprisonment.
In a word:

Attack

TRUTH PRINCIPLE
Expectations = Attack

Here are some examples of how the program uses neutral things
To attack and imprison you.

GIVING TO GET

GIVE	GET
Pay for dinner	*So you can GET them To pay next time*
Take them out this time	*So you can GET them to take you out next time*
Give them a kiss	*So you can GET a kiss*
Give them a hug	*So you can GET a hug*
Send them a text	*So you can GET a response text*
Call them and leave a message	*So you can GET them To call you back*
Express your dissatisfaction And anger with them	*So you can GET them to change*
Express your feelings	*So you can GET their validation*
Spend time with them	*So you can GET them to spend Time with you*

What are these?

These are all expressions of imprisonment and attack.
Whenever you do something with the expectation of anything in return,

Even a *"thank you"* –

You are attacking and imprisoning your partner and yourself.

101

LOVE GIFTS
Free to Give and Free to Receive

What is a gift?
A gift is something that is Freely given and Freely received.
Love gives gifts, not expectations. Love gives Freely, not to get.
Love does not give someone a gift
And then tell them how to receive the gift,
Or even to receive it at all.
If they do choose to receive it,
Love will not tell them what to do with it after they receive it.
The gift is theirs now,
And they do what they want to do with it.

RECIPROCITY
Your Relationship is not a Business Transaction

The program teaches that reciprocity is Love.
Reciprocity is NOT Love.
Reciprocity is a game.
In games you keep score. Love does not keep score.

Reciprocity says:
I do for you, you do for me.
I scratch your back, you scratch my back.
So if I ask you for something, you are supposed to give it to me.
You owe me.

Love says:
I am Free and so are you.
I do what I want to do, and I don't do what I don't want to do.

If you ask me to scratch your back and I want to, I will be Happy to do it.
I consider it my gift to you. I expect nothing in return.
You owe me nothing.

If you want to scratch my back, please do! I am Happy to receive it.
I know it is your gift to me because it is what you want to do.
*You are expecting nothing in return, because **I don't owe you anything.***

We are Free to do what we want to do.

THE BEAUTY IN FREEDOM
Choosing to Love, Each and Every Time

Here is the Beauty in being Free, and being with someone who is Free.
The Beauty is,
You know that you could be doing absolutely anything you want to do,
And of all of those things, you choose to be with them.
You also know that they could be doing absolutely anything,
And they choose to be with you.

You don't *have* to be with them, and they don't *have* to be with you.
You are not cellmates in prison. You *choose* to be together –
Each and every time.

You don't have to Love them, and they don't have to Love you.
You *choose* to Love each other –
Each and every time.

You don't owe them anything and they don't owe you anything,
Yet you *choose* to gift each other with
Attention, Affection, Adoration and Appreciation.

On the other hand –
How would you like to be with someone who was with you
Only because they were afraid of what would happen if they were not?

Or someone who got you a gift,
Only because they were afraid of what would happen if they didn't?

This is guilt, which is an expression of fear.
Guilt is imprisonment.
If you feel guilty about something,

Don't do it.

Love is Freedom.
Love is Beautiful.

Therefore,
Freedom is Beautiful.

EXERCISE
Calling and Texting

Don't be a "call me back" person

What is the purpose of this exercise?

The purpose of this exercise is to use your phone interactions
With your partner as a reminder that you are both Free.

This is a simple ongoing exercise you can do with your partner to help
Support each other's Freedom, and deprogram some common expectations
That come up in relationships around phones.

TEXTING WITH LOVE
Text When You Want To

- If you text your partner, only text them when you want to text them
- Don't text them "back" just because they sent you a text first, unless you want to text them
- Don't expect them to text you back within a particular time frame
- Know that they will text you when they want to

CALLING WITH LOVE
Don't be a "Call Me Back" Person

- If you call your partner, you called them because you want to speak to them
- If they don't answer when you called – they are unavailable
- Choose to leave them a message or don't leave them a message – do what you want
- If you choose to leave a message, tell them you'll talk to them later
- **DO NOT** TELL THEM TO **"CALL ME BACK WHEN YOU GET THE MESSAGE!"**

Why not?

Because your relationship is not a business,
And your partner's phone is not a customer service hotline.

104

That's why.
If you are not in a business relationship,
Your partner doesn't owe you ANYTHING –
Including a call back.
They call you when they want to.
Even if they saw your caller ID and ignored it, they can do that too.
Why?
Because they are Free.
That's why.

If you really want to talk to them, call them again.
Do not be attached to the outcome.
If and when they call you, it is because they wanted to.
Since you are both expressing Freedom, which is Love –
You should only *want* to talk to them when they really *want* to talk to you.

If you have set the goal for Love in your relationship,
You have nothing to be concerned about.
Your relationship is real, and nothing real can be threatened.
Even by a missed call.

Do not put obligations and expectations on your partner
To do anything for you.
What they do is always their choice.
Obligations and expectations cause guilt.

Practice with Everyone
This exercise can extend into all of your relationships with
Anyone you talk with on the phone.
They do not even have to be aware that you are doing it.

Just remember, when you leave a message:

Don't be a "call me back" person.

Talk to them later.

Call them until you reach them.

And you do what you want to do.

PART 3
RELATIONSHIP MATTERS

What is this Part of the Manual about?

In this final part, we will discuss:
- Common relationship topics and themes
- Questions that often come up in relationships
- Answers that represent BOTH thought systems covered in Part 2
  - *How does Love see this?*
  - *How does the program see this?*
- Another way of looking at things

You are encouraged have a conversation about each of these topics.

Remember:
Every topic is two topics
Why?
Because we are looking at **TWO thought systems.**
Love and the program (fear).

Therefore, in discussing any of these topics,
We are discussing two entirely different ways of seeing them.

In discussing both ways of seeing,
We are continuing to bring clarity to the questions:

How does Love operate in Relationships?

How does the program operate in Relationships?

Ready?

Let's Begin.

CHAPTER 10
FULL APPRECIATION
You Want to be Fully Appreciated

What if there was ONE answer to EVERY problem that
Arises in your relationship?
Would you want to know what that answer is?
What if this answer works all the time, and never fails?
Would you use it?
What if you had something that everyone wants all the time?
Would you offer it?

What is the key to resolving problems quickly,
And restoring the Love in your relationship?

It comes down to one word:

Appreciation.

What is Appreciation?

Appreciation is an expression of Love.
Appreciation is Love expressed as Gratitude,
Loving thoughts, and Conscious Consideration of each other.

Why is Appreciation the answer to every problem?

When you forget the goal and purpose of your relationship,
(Meaning, when you forget Love),
Genuine Appreciation aligns you with your goal instantly.

No matter what you are going through, Appreciation is always the answer.
Appreciation is always right on time,
And everyone wants to be Appreciated.
The good news is also that Appreciation can be used AT ANY TIME,
Not only when the program comes up.

Appreciate each other.
You want to be Fully Appreciated.
Your partner wants to be Fully Appreciated.
So, Appreciate each other, Fully.

It does not matter what you are Appreciating about each other.

Appreciation is Appreciation.

You can ALWAYS find something to Appreciate about each other.

IMPORTANT
When is the most important time to express Appreciation?

When you don't want to.

Meaning, when the program is running.
When you are not feeling Peace,
And when your partner is not feeling Peace.

Appreciating your partner when you are feeling upset is not always
Going to be easy,
Which is why you should get in the habit of doing it.
When?
When you **ARE** feeling Peace.

Why do this?
By Appreciating your partner, especially during times of emotional strain,
You are *asking* for what you truly want in that moment, which is Love.
You are asking for Love by giving Love.
If you are giving Love, that must mean you already have it to give.
By giving it you are reminding each other of your
Goal and Purpose for being together,
Which is Love.

How do you do it?
We've covered a lot in this Manual about how to identify the program
And how it operates.
Now that you know all about that, wouldn't it be nice to know:

How to shut the program down?
How to activate Love in your relationship?

Appreciation actually activates Love and blocks the program (fear)
At the same time.
Remember, you can only have either Love or fear
In your conscious awareness at any given time.
So anything that activates one guidance system, MUST block the other.
Listening to Love blocks the program,
Listening to the program blocks Love.

Since this is a Manual about Love, the answer is simple,
Because Love is simple.

Here are a couple of principles to help you understand how problems
Are viewed by Love and by the program.

LOVE PRINCIPLE
Love has only ONE Answer for EVERY Problem, EVERY Time

PROGRAM PRINCIPLE
The program has Many Different Answers for Every Problem,
Every Time

Loves sees everything as one, so Love sees no separateness.
The program sees everything and everyone as separate.

How does the program "solve" problems?
The program would "solve" a problem through
Fragmentation and compartmentalization.

What does that mean?
It means that the program would first have you isolate yourself –
(From your partner, from Love, from the Truth),
Then analyze and separate out parts of the "problem",
And attempt to deal with each part separately.
This is how the program makes everything seem very complicated.

How does Love solve problems?

Firstly, Love does not see a "problem" at all.
The only problem you have is that you **THINK** there is a problem.
Love understands that every problem comes from blocking Love,
And sees the "problem" as an opportunity to extend Love.

According to the program, the problem is always something
Or someone outside of you.
The program will point to whoever is nearest to you
As the source of the problem,
And who would that be in your relationship?
Your partner.

Which is why it would have you separate from them
To "solve" the "problem" you *think* you have WITH them, alone.

This is inter-dimensional ignorance.
Don't listen to it.

So what is Love's one answer?

Love.

Love's only answer is always *to Love.*

Appreciation is an expression of Love.
Any expression of Love contains the FULL content of Love.
When you express Appreciation, you are Fully expressing Love.

APPRECIATE ALWAYS
Appreciate in All Ways

Appreciation should not *only* be given when conflict arises.
Appreciation can be given at any time,
And should be given as often as possible.

Reminding your partner of your Love for them
In moments of fear is not always easy, but it is *always* worth it.

Why isn't it easy to express Appreciation (at first)?

Because when the program is running,
You are NOT thinking Loving thoughts about your partner.
You are thinking the program's thoughts about your partner.
Which means you will not have Peace.

And make no mistake about it –

The program hates you, and the program hates your partner.

Most of all, the program hates Love and Peace.
The program wants you to be a source of conflict and pain for each other,
Not a source of Appreciation and Peace for each other.

110

What are the program's thoughts on Appreciation?

The program is totally unaware of the concept of "Appreciation".

...And that's the end of that conversation.

Moving on.

APPRECIATION APPLICATION
Gift Your Partner with Appreciation

Appreciation is always a gift.
It is never forced, it is never held back.
Appreciation is always Freely given and Freely received.
Express Appreciation in your Loving relationship as often as possible
And never hold it back.
Use everything at your disposal as a means
To deliver Appreciation to your partner.
Such as...

Gifts, words, notes, calls, texts, acts, etc.

Before we go into your Appreciation Assignment,
Let's take a look at the two ways of expressing Appreciation.

What are the two ways of expressing Appreciation?

1. **Universal Appreciation**
2. **Specific Appreciation**

What is Universal Appreciation?

Universal Appreciation is acknowledging and Appreciating someone's
Very existence and presence.
Universal Appreciation can be expressed to anyone at any time
And still be True.

What is the most common form of Universal Appreciation?

A simple
"Thank you"

Examples of Universal Appreciation:

Thank you
I Appreciate you
I Love you

Universal Appreciation is for everyone.
Universal Appreciation is the way Love sees everyone.
You don't even have to know someone to
Give them Universal Appreciation.

What is Specific Appreciation?

Specific Appreciation is when you
Appreciate specific things about someone.
It is when you Appreciate the things they did and said
That are meaningful to you.
It is when you express your gratitude for how they
PERSONALLY impacted your life.

Example:

Thank you for your thoughtful card
Thank you for picking me up from the airport
I really enjoyed the meal you prepared
I Love when you sing to me
Thank you for your advice about _____
I Appreciate your input

When you gift your partner specific Appreciation,
You thank them for the moments, memories and experiences
That only the two of you share.

You may ask:
So which is better? Universal, or specific Appreciation?

Appreciation is Appreciation.
Appreciation is Love and Love is always Maximal.

So do it.

Communicate, Congratulate, Participate, Appreciate.

Why are we covering both ways of Appreciation?

Simple:

So you can use both!

How do you use Universal Appreciation?

The key to Universal Appreciation is simply to **GIVE THANKS.**

Say "Thank You".
Give your partner thanks *"just because…"*
You don't really need a reason.
The fact that they are there is reason enough.
Acknowledge them every chance you have.

How do you use specific Appreciation?

The key to specific Appreciation is this:

Appreciate Individual Acts.

Think of anything your partner *ever* did for you that you are grateful for.
Think of moments, memories, and experiences that brought you both Love.
Share those thoughts, moments, memories, and experiences together again.

APPRECIATION ASSIGNMENT
Written and Spoken Appreciation

It's time to apply what you've learned.

When?

Right now.

Follow these instructions:

1. Take out your dedicated notebooks.
2. At the top of a new page, write your partner's name.
3. Beneath their name, write five or more things you Appreciate about them.
    a. Be sure to combine Universal and specific Appreciation.
        i. It does not need to be in any kind of order.

b. Use these questions to guide you:
   i. ***What do you Appreciate about them?***
   ii. ***What is something they do or have done that you Appreciate?***
   iii. ***What is something they say or have said that you Appreciate?***
   iv. ***Why are you grateful they are in your life?***

4. When you are both finished, exchange, and read it aloud to each other.
   a. If you are not able to exchange right now, read what you wrote aloud to your partner.
      i. *By the way, it's okay either way.*

EXAMPLE

<u>"Partner's name"</u>
I Appreciate you for being in my life.
I am grateful we met.
Thank you for helping me look for my keys when I misplaced them.
Thank you for always reminding me to drink water.
Thank you for texting me earlier to tell me you were thinking about me.
I Appreciate how attentive you are to me.
I Love when you listen to my ideas.
Thank you for reading this Manual "Love is Not a Game" with me,
And doing the exercises with me.
I Love you.

In Conclusion:
This is a very simple assignment.
It should not take you many, many years to do.
If you start today, you will finish today.
If you don't start today, you may not start tomorrow.
So do it **NOW**.

Because...

If you don't Appreciate now,
When will you?

If you don't Appreciate right here,
Where will you?

If you don't Appreciate each other,
Who will Appreciate YOU?

Start now
This is not a game.

CHAPTER 11

ATTRACTION?
Stimulation, Polarity, Chemistry

Let's have an interaction about attraction.

Just to be clear, when the word "attraction" is used in this chapter,
We are talking about physical, sexual attraction.
Let's begin.

What is Attraction?

"Attraction" is another word for "polarity" or "chemistry"
Between two people.
Attraction is natural.
It's normal to experience attraction.

What is attraction NOT?
Attraction is NOT Love.
Love has nothing to do with attraction.
Attraction is not good or bad, right or wrong.
Attraction is neutral. It has no inherent meaning.
Attraction can only have the meaning you give it in your relationship.

Why is attraction not Love?

Attraction can be threatened.
Love cannot be threatened.

Anything that can be threatened does not mean anything.
Anything that can change does not mean anything.
Attraction can be threatened.
Attraction changes.
Attraction doesn't mean anything.

The only thing that means anything is Love.
Love means Everything.
Love cannot be threatened,
And Love does not change.

What does the program teach about attraction?

The program has a very superficial way of looking at things.

Remember, attraction is *NOT* a Universal Principle.
What does that mean?
That means attraction will NOT give you the same results
With every single person every time.
And if it cannot be relied on to produce the same results every time,
It is *totally* unreliable.

The program believes that attraction is Love.
Why?
The program mistakes attraction for Love because of
How *stimulated* you feel by it.
The program believes when you are feeling stimulated by your attraction –
You are feeling Love.
This is not so.

The Truth is:
You can be *madly* attracted to someone who hates you,
And you can have zero attraction for someone who
Loves you totally and completely.

Remember:
Purpose determines meaning.
How many purposes do you have to decide from?
Two.
How many guides do you have to follow?
Two.
What are they?
Love or the program (fear).

The real question is:
How will you use attraction?

If you use your attraction to try to *GET* something from someone –
Which guide are you listening to?

If you both use attraction to join and extend Love,
Appreciation, Care, and Trust to each other –
Which guide are you listening to?

Attraction, just like any feeling is just an experience.
It doesn't mean anything.
You give attraction all the meaning it has,
By deciding the *purpose* you will use it for.

WHAT IS ATTRACTION FOR?
Joining in Love

You cannot help who you are attracted to,
But you can help your programming.

Attraction is not Love,
Although you can use your attraction to each other to join in Love.
Your attraction to your partner is just icing on the cake.

The program would use your attraction to sabotage you.
Love would use your attraction to Heal you.

You cannot change the fact that you will experience attraction.
That's like trying to change your genetic makeup.
You can pretend you don't experience attraction,
But attraction is natural.
You cannot fight nature and win.

So Don't.
Just Don't.

What you want to remember is this:
The sensation of attraction and being "turned on" by someone
Is just a sensation.
It doesn't mean anything.
You decide what you will DO with it.

Will you use your attraction to stimulate your desire to GET?
Or will you use attraction to join in Love?

If you are attracted to each other,
That means you already **WANT** to join.

So why not use that joining to Love each other?

Let's take a deeper look at how both
Love and the program use attraction.

ATTRACTION

PROGRAM'S USE OF ATTRACTION	LOVE'S USE OF ATTRACTION
The program uses your attraction to Enter into a relationship that has no Purpose and no direction.	Love uses your attraction to Establish a relationship based on a Common Purpose and a Common Curriculum.
The program uses your attraction to Try to *get* Love from your partner.	Love uses your attraction to *Give and receive* (gift) Love to Each other.
The program uses your attraction to Try to get your partner to fulfill Your imagined needs.	Love uses your attraction to Help you realize that you are both Already whole, And to join in wholeness together.
The program uses your attraction to Deepen your emotional wounds.	Love uses your attraction to Heal Your emotional wounds.
The program uses your attraction to Keep you coming back to a situation That you know will not get better.	Love uses your attraction to inspire You to continue joining in a Relationship that *only* gets better.
The program uses your attraction to Get you to repeat the same insane Thought patterns and toxic behavior That will result in pain.	Love uses your attraction to bring You together to recognize and *Break* the insane thought patterns And toxic behavior forever.
The program uses your attraction to Guide you to a partner and Relationship that you will use to Hurt and victimize yourself.	Love uses your attraction to guide You to a partner who only wants to Join in Love with you.
CONCLUSION	
When you are operating from The program, You will use your attraction to your Partner to hurt yourself.	When you are operating from Love, You will use your attraction for Each other to Join in a Loving, Healing and Happy relationship.

BEING IRRESISTIBLE TO EACH OTHER
True Attraction

You can resist temptation and you can resist attraction,
But you cannot resist Love.

How do you become totally irresistible?

When you truly Love someone, and they truly Love you,
You become *irresistible* to each other.
This is a **much** greater Attraction than your
Physical attraction for each other.
Why?
Because of the unlimited Love you radiate to each other.
So...
If you really want to be irresistible to your partner,
Love them.

This is True Attraction.
The Attraction of Love.

ABOUT YOUR BODY...
An Ice Cream Cone

Your body will not look, feel, or smell the same 60 years from now.
Which means that your body changes, and your body can be threatened.
If you rely on the attractiveness of your body to feel Loved,
You will lose.
You can only lose when you're doing what?
Playing games.

You are entitled to Love –
Now.
And all the time.

Just remember,
Your body is like an ice cream cone...

It's melting.

Better enjoy it while it lasts.

CHAPTER 12

COMMITMENT?
What About Commitment?

Are you in a committed relationship?
Are you committed to Love?

Let's start with this question:
What is Commitment?

<u>TRUTH PRINCIPLE</u>
Commitment is Neutral

In reality, commitment is neutral.
Commitment itself doesn't mean anything.
The meaning comes from the PURPOSE you give to it.
How so?
You can be committed to Loving someone,
Or you can be committed to strangling them the next time you see them.
Commitment is not good or bad, right or wrong.
Commitment is just another tool at your disposal.
How you use commitment is for you to *decide.*

You have the power of decision.

Ask yourself:
How will I use commitment?
Will I use commitment in the service of Love?
Or to perpetuate the painful program?

Let's take a deeper look into how both the program
And Love look at commitment.

How does the program view commitment?

<u>PROGRAM PRINCIPLE</u>
Commitment Means Time

The program believes that commitment = **time in.**

This is clearly a game.

Why is it a game?

*Because **time in** also means what?*
Time out.

Only the program measures time in relationships,
Because it thinks time means something.

The program will say things such as:

*"We're in a committed relationship.
We've been together for 10 years."*

The program believes that the amount of time you have
Invested in a relationship matters,
Even if there is no evidence of Peace and Happiness
To be found in the relationship.

What does time mean?

Time itself means nothing.
It is the purpose you use it for that gives time its meaning.

Can time be depended on?
No.

Why?
Because it can be threatened.

How?
Because it changes

When?
All the time!

Does Love change?
Love never changes.
Not at any time.

What is Love's view on commitment?

LOVE PRINCIPLE
Love Is Totally Committed All the Time

Love has nothing to do with time.
And time has nothing to do with commitment.

Remember,
Love transcends time.
You can Love someone you've never spent any time with.
You can hate someone you've known for your entire life.

PROGRAM PRINCIPLE
The More Time you spend in a Relationship,
The More your Love grows

The program teaches:

"The more time we spend together
The deeper our Love becomes"

To the program a relationship becomes more valuable and more Loving
The more *time* you invest in it.
This is simply not True.
Why?
Because Love is maximal all the time.
When you are committed to Love,
Your commitment is maximal all the time.

LOVE PRINCIPLE
Love Operates NOW

Love transcends time because Love operates in the present.
The present is NOW.

"Now" is not an interval of time.

You can be together for 60 years and not Love each other,
Or you can be together for 60 minutes and be Fully
Present with each other in every moment.

Which one is Love?
Which one is Truly meaningful?

Commitment has nothing to do with how long you've been
In a relationship with someone.

Love asks:
What are you committed to right now?

PROGRAM PRINCIPLE
You can only be in one committed relationship at a time

The program believes that you are in a committed relationship if you
Are giving someone the majority of your time.
Even if, in that time, you are not experiencing Love.

This is because the program is committed to form and not content.

To the program, commitment operates along linear time.
It believes that:
More time = more commitment.

Since time can be measured, it believes commitment can also be measured.
But a measurement means a scoreboard.
And a scoreboard means what?

It's a game.

According to the program's twisted logic:
Your time is limited,
And commitment is measured by time-in a relationship,
Therefore you can only be Fully committed to one person
And one relationship at a time.

This is limitation and insanity.

LOVE PRINCIPLE
Love is Totally Committed to Everyone, All the Time

Love cannot be threatened.
If you are totally committed to Love,
That means you are totally committed to Loving everyone who you are in
Any kind of relationship with.

124

When you are totally committed to Love,
Your relationships will not conflict with each other in any way.
The belief that you can only be committed to one person,
Or one relationship at a time –
Is insane.

Why doesn't Love have anything to do with time?

Time can be threatened. Love cannot be threatened.
You can run out of time.
You cannot run out of Love.
Time includes levels and intervals.

In short:

Time is a game.

Games operate on a timer.
Any relationship that operates on a timer is a game.

Who's watching the clock?

Not Love.

The program asks disorienting questions such as:

"How long have you been together?"
"Where is this relationship going?"
"Are you in a committed relationship?"

The only question that really matters is Love's question:

"Do you Love each other RIGHT NOW, in this moment?"

TRUE COMMITMENT
Committed to Love

Your True commitment has to do with your commitment to
Loving in this present moment.
Love does not count the days, weeks, months and years
Of one relationship, and measure them against
The days, weeks, months, and years of any other relationship.

A relationship is valuable to you only if the relationship is
Committed to Love.

Love is totally committed to everything and everyone all the time.

LET'S PUT THIS MATTER TO REST

Your only commitment should be to Love.
The only thing you CAN be totally committed to
That won't change is Love.
Therefore, if you Love someone,
If you Love ANYONE,
You ARE in a committed relationship with them.
Whether you know them for a day or for a lifetime.
Love is total and complete.
Love is maximal all the time.

So once again:

Are you in a committed relationship?

You **ARE** in a committed relationship.

How?

Your relationship is committed to Love.

CHAPTER 13

COMPROMISE AND SACRIFICE?
Doing What You Don't Want To Do

What is compromise and sacrifice?
For the purposes of this chapter,
"Compromise" and "sacrifice" mean exactly the same thing,
And the terms will be used interchangeably.

We will cover how the program uses compromise and sacrifice,
And then we will cover how Love uses it.

Let's Begin.

What do these terms mean?

To compromise or sacrifice means to **lose**.
If you are losing, you are doing what?

Playing games.

The program teaches that you are always compromising what you want
For the sake of some greater good.
The program believes that compromise is necessary in a relationship
If you want the relationship to work.

The program says:
You have to compromise in this relationship if you want it to work.
You are not both going to like the same things.
You are not both going to want to do the same things.
You have to find a middle-ground.
If you want this relationship to work, you gotta give a little to GET a little.

This is a lie.

Essentially, the program is telling you
That you have to lose in order to gain.
This makes sense only if you are totally insane.

Again, if you are losing at any time,
What must that mean?

It means you are playing games.

Love would never *require* you to lose to gain.
Love doesn't experience lack or loss,
So Love doesn't want to GET anything.

Love is Free.
Love wants only what is Freely given, and Freely received.

What does Love say about compromise?

Love says this:
**You do what you want to do,
And you don't do what you don't want to do.
You are Free.**

Following the program's logic –
When you compromise, you are settling.
You are settling for less than what you want.
You are doing something you don't want to do.
Your are *reluctantly* going along with something
In the hopes that you can GET what you want
At the end of the road.

That road leads to only one outcome:

Relationship wreck.

*Why should you ever settle for less than what you want?
What do you truly want?*

You want to Love, and to be Loved.

Love teaches that you should only be asking for one thing, at all times.

What should you be asking for?

Everything.

What is Everything?

Love is Everything.

Why do you have the right to ask for Everything?

Because that is what you are offering.
You are offering Love.

If you do something because you WANT to –
You are never sacrificing.

TWO EXAMPLES

The following are two situations that may or may not involve sacrifice.
Your job is to determine which one is rooted in
Sacrifice and compromise (loss),
And which one is rooted in Love.

Example 1:

A parent wants to provide for their children.
This parent does not have a lot of money.
They work long hours at multiple low-paying jobs,
Because that's what it takes to provide for their children.
They are Happy to provide for their children.

Example 2:

A parent has children who they do not want to provide for.
This parent is extremely financially wealthy. They do not work.
This parent only provides for their children because they would suffer
Severe legal consequences if they didn't.
Although money is not an issue,
They feel bitter and resentful whenever they
Have to provide for their children.

Of the two examples,

Which parent is sacrificing, and which one is not?

The program wants you to think that it is the parent
In the first example who is sacrificing.

They question is:
Are they losing?

They are doing what they want to do,
Which is to provide for their children.

They are doing what they Truly want to do.

The parent in the second example is sacrificing,

Why?

Because they are **LOSING their Peace** every time they **think** about
Providing for their children.

Even though they can easily afford to do everything that is
Required of them on the level of form,
Their content is still sacrifice.
They still feel *loss.*

They are doing what they do not Truly want to do.

Think about this...
Do you really want to be with a partner who is with you ONLY because:

They think they HAVE to be with you?
They don't think they can do "better" than you,
So they "settle" for this relationship with you?
They are afraid of what people would think if you broke up?
They only want what they are GETTING from you,
But they don't really want **YOU?**
They are afraid of how you would react if they told you
How they really felt?

You don't really WANT to be with someone
Who is with you because they feel they *have* to be –
For ANY reason.

You want to be with someone who Loves you exactly as you are,
And you want to Love them exactly as they are.

SACRIFICING FOR LOVE
Losing your fear

For everything the program uses, Love has a better use.
So the question we will now ask is:

How would Love use sacrifice?

Remember, to sacrifice and compromise is to experience loss.
Love is Everything, so Love cannot lose.
You can still *feel* the feeling of loss though –
And remember, feelings are not good or bad.

What are feelings?

Feelings are experiences.
You can use ALL of your experiences in the service of Love.

So how can you use the feeling of loss
To increase your awareness of Love?

If you're going to feel like you're "losing" something –

Feel yourself *losing* your doubts and fears.
Feel yourself *losing* your attraction to the program.
Feel yourself *losing* your pain.

Those are the things you want to lose.
Those are the things you should sacrifice.

Remember Love
Loss is not good or bad. Sacrifice is not good or bad,
It is either helpful, or unhelpful.
As we explored, you *can* sacrifice for Love,
By losing your fear.
This is how Love uses sacrifice.

The program wants you to feel like you've lost your Love.
It wants you to sacrifice Love to gain something else.
Since Love is everything, by listening to the program,
You always gain nothing.

Can you lose Love?
It is not possible to lose Love. Love is what you are.
It is not possible to lose yourself, but you can forget who you are.

In other words…
It is possible to lose your ***awareness*** of Love.
It is possible to forget Love.

When you forget Love, you forget everything that comes with Love,
And you experience what it would be like without it.
When you forget Love, you forget:
Peace, Appreciation, Trust, Happiness, Joy, Freedom, Fun, etc.

Which is why the goal is always to
Remember Love.

CHAPTER 14
FALLING IN LOVE?
Falling Out of Love

You have heard the phrase "falling in Love" before.
Now it's time to take a look at what it means.

What does it mean to "fall in Love"?

Both the program and Love have different
Understandings of what it means to
"Fall in Love".

How does the program see falling in Love?

The program always relates the idea and experience
Of falling in Love to an intimate partner.
Why?
Because the program sees Love as special.
You cannot just fall in Love with anyone, because it's a rare thing.
Therefore, falling in Love is something special,
And if you're lucky you can experience it once or twice in your life.

What happens after you fall in Love?
As with everything that the program enters into,
It must end.
And it must end in misery and doom.
The program cannot conceive of falling in Love without eventually
"Falling out of Love".

How does Love see falling in Love?

Falling hurts.
According to Love, the whole *"falling"* part is completely unnecessary.
Unless we are talking about the seasons,
To fall means you've had an accident.
Love is not blind, and Love doesn't have accidents.
Love *Joins in Love* from a state of Full Awareness and Consciousness.

You are IN Love already.
You are already IN Love because you already ARE Love.
You partner is already IN Love because they already ARE Love.
When you *Join IN Love* together,

You are just becoming aware of the Love you already share.

When you both become aware of the Love you already have,
You begin to experience that Love together.

How does it feel to Join in Love with someone?

Joining in Love feels Awesome!
How do you feel?
You feel Curious - you want to know more about them.
You feel Drawn - you feel attracted to them.
You feel like Joining - you want to join with them.
You feel Excitement - you have fun together.

This is a normal experience.

According to Love:
"Falling in Love" means "Joining in Love"
And Joining in Love is not special.
When you fall you hurt yourself.

How do you "fall in Love"?

It may come as a surprise but,
When you have the experience of "falling in Love" with someone,
The Love you feel for each other *IS TRUE LOVE.*
True Love is the absence of the program (fear).

That is why it is so powerful.

There are feelings of:
Excitement, Curiosity, wanting to Join, Willingness,
Appreciation, Freedom, Fun,
And not being attached to a specific outcome.

All of that content IS LOVE.

So how does the program try to sabotage your relationship at this point?

Here's how:

After falling in Love,
You're probably thinking along these lines:

You *[thinking to yourself]:*
This experience is great! I Love it!
I Love being with this person!
This relationship is such a pleasure!

The program *[enters your mind and whispers]:*
I know right?
What if it could be this way ALL the time?
Wouldn't you like that?

You *[interested]:*
Of course! I would Love that.
But I'm not worried about it.
I'm just going to enjoy this experience and let things be.

The program *[still whispering]:*
No, no, no...
You should be worried. You could get hurt.
You don't want to get hurt do you?

You *[wondering why it's saying these things, and why it's whispering]:*
Of course not.

The program *[knows it has your attention because you're talking to it]:*
I wouldn't want you to get hurt either...
But I can protect you.
You just have to Trust me.

You *[getting worried and afraid]:*
How can you help me?

The program *[not whispering anymore]:*
Listen...
If you want this relationship to keep bringing you Happiness,
You CAN'T just let it be.
If you want this partner to keep bringing you Happiness,
You CAN'T just let them be.
You have to take control!
You have to control the form of this relationship so it never changes.
You have to make rules and scripts for how your partner should behave
So they never change.
You have to make sure nothing happens that would expose
Your own insecurities and fears.

You have to reserve a part of yourself from them so you don't get hurt.
If they do something you don't like,
You have to make them feel guilty and punish them.
That's the ONLY way you'll control them and keep them!
That's the only way you'll keep this relationship and keep this Love!

You *[now asking for the program's misguidance]:*
What if I don't do this?

The program *[speaking quite confidently now]:*
You will lose them.
I promise you.
You will lose this relationship.
I promise you.
You will lose all the Love and Happiness you are feeling right now.
I promise you.
And you will get hurt.
I promise you.

You *[not wanting to believe this insanity, but still believing out of fear]:*
. . . .

The program *[takes your silence as consent, picks up a microphone]:*
I'm telling you, the only way you can KEEP this Love
Is TO CONTROL IT!
Which means you have to control them.
By any means necessary.

You *[indecisive, but still listening]:*
. . . .

The program *[knows it has you right where it wants you]:*
This Love is special! It may never ever come again.
Will you just let it slip through your fingers like that?

You *[scared]:*
No...I don't want to lose this Love...
What should I do???

The program *[putting on its sunglasses]:*
Let me tell you...

This is the beginning of the end.

Don't listen to the program's lies.
As long as you are listening to the program,
You are not listening to Love.
Everything the program says is a lie,
Designed to deceive.

TRUTH PRINCIPLE
What You Try To Keep You Lose.
What You Free you keep.

The way to "keep" Love is not to try to control it.
The way to "keep" Love in your relationship is by *Freeing.*
Freeing how?
Freeing your relationship from the program's scripts.
Freeing your partner from the program's scripts.
Freeing yourself from the program's scripts
Being Free of the program's lies.

All the program does is imprison.
If you want Freedom, *Free them.*

How does the program sabotage relationships?

Now we're going to look at what happens step-by-step.

Remember,
You and your partner are the same.
You have the same program.
So if it's running in one of you, it's running in both of you.

FALLING IN LOVE - FALLING OUT OF LOVE
The Breakdown

Here is the falling in-and-out of Love ritual:

The relationship starts off as TRUE LOVE.
True Love feels GOOD, and naturally you want that feeling to continue.
(True Love is experienced in the absence of the program).
The program enters.

It tells you lies, and tries to scare you into believing
That the Love won't last.
It tells you the only way the Love will last is if you have control –
Control over your partner,
And control over the form of the relationship.
You listen to the program and react out of **fear of loss.**

GAME START
You are afraid you will lose your relationship.
You are afraid you will lose your partner,
And ultimately you are afraid you will lose the Love you have and want.
You listen to the program.
You imprison your partner and yourself with programmatic
Scripts and expectations.
These scripts and expectations put unbearable strain on your relationship.
Why?
Because you and your partner are both naturally FREE.
The strain turns into emotional pain when the scripts fail to be maintained.
You project attack and blame on your partner for your emotional pain.
No one takes responsibility for their feelings or for their experience.
This produces an adversarial and emotionally hostile environment.
Your partner is now seen as your opponent, or enemy.
You behave like enemies.
What do enemies do?
Enemies have fights, arguments and conflict.
This eventually results in harsh separation – on bad terms.
GAME OVER

FYI
This is a ritual (or pattern) of the program, so it is predictable.
This programmatic pattern will continue to repeat until it is healed.
You will repeat it in different relationships with different partners,
Or you will repeat it in the same relationship with the same partner.
The point being –
If you continue listening to the program, *it will repeat.*
It will continue to repeat until this pattern is healed.

There is a way to heal from all of this.
How?

STOP!
Just stop.

Stop
Listening to the program.

Stop
Reacting in fear.

Stop
Playing games.

Stop
Blocking Love.

Just stop.

Honeymoon "Phase"
It's A Game

The program teaches that the experience of falling in Love is special,
And usually short-lived.

It calls this the *"honeymoon phase"* of a relationship.

Let's be clear...
There are no phases in a relationship dedicated to Love.
A phase is an interval of time.

And where do you have time intervals?

In games.

In a Loving relationship,
You are either Loving each other, or you are forgetting to.
It's that simple.

If you decide *"honeymoon"* means *"Loving"*,
Your relationship can ALWAYS be experienced as a honeymoon –

If you both decide you want it to be.

BEING IN LOVE

Or not

To conclude on this topic of "falling in Love",
Remember that when you are IN Love, there is nowhere to fall.
Falling hurts.
Whether you fall in or you fall out,
You're still falling, which means it was accidental.
Love is Consciousness, not passiveness.
Love does not have "accidents".
Love does not fall, Love flows.

Decide
Decide to join IN Love, or not.

How do you know you are in Love?

When you feel like joining with your partner, you are in Love.
When you feel like being separate, you are not in Love.
When you feel Happy about your relationship, you are in Love.
When you are feeling upset about your relationship, you are not in Love.

THERE WILL BE NO MORE CONFUSION ON THIS:

If at any time you are experiencing Loving feelings with ANY PERSON,
You are literally *IN LOVE* with them.
When you are not feeling those qualities, you are not in Love.
You are forgetting to Love.
Period.

Stop playing games,
Decide.

CHAPTER 15
FORGIVENESS?

Forgiveness has ABSOLUTELY NOTHING to do with them,
And ABSOLUTELY EVERYTHING to do with YOU

Let's talk about forgiveness.
It happens.

What is forgiveness?

Forgiveness is a way of seeing.
There are two entirely different ways of seeing
That are called "forgiveness."
One of these ways is offered by the program –
So you already know it's a lie.

The other way is how Love sees forgiveness.
So you already know it's the Truth.
One way is based entirely on guilt.
The other way is based entirely on Innocence.

PROGRAMMATIC FORGIVE-MESS
It's a Mess

How does the program see forgiveness?

To the program, forgiveness is ALWAYS for someone else,
And about someone else.
According to the program: to *"forgive"* means to *"pardon"*.
When forgiveness is required, it means someone is guilty.

What happened?

They have wronged you in some way,
You condemn them for the wrong, and you hold a grievance against them.

You feel justified in your anger at them, because they hurt you.
You are the victim. They are the perpetrator.

How would the program have you "forgive" someone?

140

Taking "The High Road"

When you "forgive" someone, you become their judge.
You have already convicted them of the crime,
And you have already judged them as guilty.
Guilt is always a request for punishment,
So you believe they DESERVE to be punished.
But since you believe you are operating from a place of moral superiority
"The high road",
You choose to overlook their wrong, and *"pardon"* them.
You may even go as far as to tell them:
"I forgive you".

What does that mean?
In your program-polluted mind,
You have just pardoned a guilty criminal.
You believe you "let them off-the-hook".
Which means you no longer require them to pay the penalty
For their crime against you.

But make no mistake about it –
They are *still guilty* for it.
Which means they are in your debt,
Because you "forgave" them.

Let's go ahead and press pause on this game now.

There are several insane premises to deconstruct here.

Let's take a look at them,
One-by-one.

Program forgiveness means:

1) **That someone is guilty.**
   a) Guilt is a byproduct of listening to the program and not listening to Love.
      i) You are not guilty. You are Innocent.
      ii) Love always sees you as Innocent.
2) **That someone actually hurt you in some way.**
   a) Take Full Responsibility for your Experience
   b) If someone didn't *physically assault your body*, or *compromise your physical health* in some way, they did nothing at all to you.
   c) The only thing hurt on you is your feelings.
      i) You are not a victim.

        (1) You feel hurt by how you choose see it.

           (a) When you see it with the program.

3) That you can judge.

  a) You CANNOT judge. It is not possible.

  b) In your mind, you can decide or believe that someone is guilty - but you cannot judge.

What would it mean to be a real judge?

    i) To be a real judge, means you would have to:

        (1) Be aware of everything regarding this person and situation

           (a) Which means every piece of information existing in the past, present, and future about them.

        (2) Be aware of what all of this information means, and how each piece interacts with every other piece.

        (3) Be in a position where you have authority over them to make a decision regarding them.

        (4) Know how your decision will affect everything and everyone involved in every way.

        (5) Be sure that you are seeing everything totally objectively with no bias, favoritism, or personal investment involved.

    ii) If you cannot do ALL OF THIS, *which you certainly cannot –* all you are doing is *making emotional conclusions based off of subjective analysis.*

    iii) If you perceive from the program, you will ALWAYS be wrong, because the program is always wrong about everything.

    iv) Again, the point here being, not that you *should not* judge, but you CANNOT judge.

  c) The only right judgment comes from Love.

    i) Love's judgment can be accessed and exercised *through* you, but not *by* you.

  d) Love is the only Authority and capable Judge in any and every circumstance.

4) That you can overlook something that did not happen.

  a) *They never hurt you in the first place, remember?*

    i) You did it to yourself.

    ii) So what are you overlooking?

5) That you are on some "higher plane" than someone else.

  a) Everyone is the same.

  b) The program would tell you that forgiving is taking the "high road."

i) This is the program's attempt ONCE AGAIN to cause separation by perceiving from a place of moral superiority and inferiority.

c) Once you have comparison – you have separation, because you are making value judgments.

    i) Values are points, and where are points used?

In games.

LOVE'S WAY OF SEEING FORGIVENESS
You are Innocent

How does Love forgive?

Actually, Love does not forgive.

What???

Again,
LOVE DOES NOT FORGIVE.

Why?

Before forgiveness can be needed in any situation,
Something else has to happen first...
This is the piece the program doesn't tell you.

What needs to happen before forgiveness is required?

Condemnation.

Condemnation is the outcome of judgment.
Condemnation is the verdict of GUILT upon someone.
And guilt is a request for punishment.

So why doesn't Love forgive?

LOVE PRINCIPLE
Love Does Not Forgive
Because Love Never Condemns

Love does not forgive because Love never condemns.

Isn't that Awesome?

Let's take a closer look:

If to "forgive" means to "pardon",
Love recognizes that there is nothing to "forgive" in the first place.
In order to forgive you must first condemn,
Which means "make guilty."
Love does not forgive because Love never makes you guilty.
Love always sees you as innocent.
There is nothing to "pardon" anyone for doing to you.
It is your own perception of things that needs to be corrected.
To "pardon" something makes it real.
Only the guilty require pardon,
And guilt is not real.
Guilt is the byproduct of listening to the program,
And the program is not real.
It does not exist at all.
The program and everything that comes from it is an illusion.
It is your *belief* in the illusion which makes it seem real to you.

The only problem you have is that you *think* there is a problem.

The only thing that needs to be forgiven, or shall we say –
Healed
Is the way you are looking at it.

LOVE'S USE OF FORGIVENESS
Healing

Just like everything else the program uses,
Love has a better use for it.

Although Love does not forgive, Love can use forgiveness.

What is Love's use of forgiveness?

To Heal.

More specifically,

To Heal your perception.

Love always starts from this position:
You are Innocent.
Everyone is Innocent.

Why?

Love Created you Innocent.

Guilt will always imprison.
Innocence will always set Free.
Although you may believe another is guilty of something,
You can only see their guilt through your guilt.
You are the same.
You can only see the program operating in someone else
If it is operating in you.
You may think you are exonerating yourself of the guilt
By projecting guilt onto someone else –
But who feels it?

You do.

<u>**PROGRAM PRINCIPLE**</u>
Guilt Is A Request For Punishment

You do not want to be imprisoned by guilt, grievances, and condemnation.
This is what the program wants.
Stop punishing yourself.

<u>**LOVE PRINCIPLE**</u>
An Innocent Mind Does Not Believe It Deserves To Suffer

Love wants you to Heal,
And Free yourself from the terrible burden of guilt.

You are not guilty!
YOU ARE INNOCENT!

How does Love want you to Heal?

Love wants you to Heal by realizing that
There is nothing to forgive.

Here's a question:

Who is forgiveness for?

Forgiveness is always for YOU.

Why?

If you are Innocent,
And you and your partner are the same,
That means they are also Innocent.

THE TRUTH
It is the way you are seeing them that is causing you pain,
NOT THEM.
It is the way you are seeing what they did or didn't do
That is causing you pain,
NOT THEM.
It is the way you are seeing what they said, or didn't say
That is causing you pain,
NOT THEM.

In short:

**It is always your own thoughts that injure you.
Not another person.**

It is your way of seeing **them**
That hurts **you.**

Ready for the good part?

Here's what you can do about it:

**You can
CHANGE YOUR MIND.**

Can you change another person?
No.
Can you change their mind?
No.
Can you change their words?
No.
Can you change their actions?
No.

What can you do?

You can change your mind about them.
You can change your mind about their words.
You can change your mind about their actions.

Ready for the best part?

They don't even have to participate!
Why?
Because the way you are thinking about them has
Absolutely NOTHING to do with them!

And guess what else?

They don't even have to be living for you to have Peace
About your relationship with them.

This is why Love's forgiveness is always about you.

How does this work in your relationship with your partner?

Adopting this way of seeing will bring enormous Peace to you
And your partner in your relationship.

How?

When you have the understanding that you and your partner are
Innocent at all times –
You will not attack each other when
The fear and programming comes up.
You will take responsibility for the way you are seeing.
You will choose to join in Healing, and Affirming each other's Innocence.
You will take your partner off the program's imaginary "hook".
You will not try to make them feel guilty for something they didn't do.

147

Clarity on this point:
When we say *"something they didn't do"* we are not talking about
The "facts" of what they actually did or said,
We're talking about *how you feel about it.*

They DID NOT make you feel the way you feel.
You did that on your own.

SEEING WITH LOVE
Forgive, and You Will See Things Differently

The way Love operates is simple.
Love operates from a place of Truth and Total Power.
As we've covered before, the Truth is:
You are responsible for how you see things.
Your thoughts, your feelings and your perceptions.

You may not be able to change the fact that you've been
Exposed to the program,
But you can choose to stop running it.
Or you can choose to let it continue to run you.
You will choose to continue to see your world through the
Harsh and distorted lens of the program,
Or you will choose to see it through the True and Gentle lens of Love.

The Truth is:
You are Powerful.
You are Capable.
You are creating your experience every single moment
By how you choose to see that moment.

Are you seeing with Love?
Or are you seeing with the program - fear?

Forgive, and you will see things differently.

CHAPTER 16
FORMS OF RELATIONSHIPS?
Dating, Open Relationships, Monogamy,
Polygamy, Marriage, Platonic, Friends, etc.

This Manual does not address the forms of relationships.
Why?
Because they do not matter whatsoever.

This is a Manual about content, not form.

The content of Love is equally applicable to all relationships,
Because Love is a Universal Truth Principle.
And the Truth is True for everyone, all the time.

There is no judgment on any form over any other.
Everyone has personal preferences.

The only thing to be said about the form,
Is that you should join in the form of relationship in which
You and your partner can allow True Love to flow Freely without fear.

If you enter into a form of relationship with fear and doubt,
Or develop *persisting* feelings of fear and doubt –
That is not the right form for you and your partner at the time.
Change it.

Change the form of the relationship,
But do not change your Goal and Purpose,
Which is to give and receive Love.

*How do you choose the **best** form of relationship?*

This is simple.
YOU do not.

Love does.

Set the Goal for Love (content),
And Trust that the Guidance of Love will show you the form.

CHAPTER 17
ROMANCE?
Romantic Gestures

Let's take a look at romance.

How does the program see romance?

The program believes that romance is an indication of Love.
It believes romantic gestures are measurements of how much
You Love your partner, and how much they Love you.
If something is being measured, it's being counted,
And where do you keep count?

In games.

What does romance mean?
Romance does not mean anything,
And romantic gestures do not indicate anything.
Why?
Because romance is form. Romance is not content.
Love is content. Fear is content.

What does this mean?
This means that just because you have romance in your relationship,
It doesn't *automatically* mean you have Love in your relationship.

What would be considered romantic gestures?

Romantic gestures are usually seen as:
Surprises, "romantic" music, poetry, cards, exotic trips, special gifts, etc.

What do romantic gestures mean?

By themselves, they all mean absolutely nothing.
You give them all the meaning they have to you.

How does this work in your relationship?
If you give Loving meanings to the romantic gestures,
Then they are in alignment with your goal -
Which is Love.

If you give them fearful meanings,

Or if you are just doing them to do them,
They are not in alignment with your Goal and Purpose.
You will give yourself fear because of them.

For example:
You can give a gift and a card to someone you hate,
And you can receive a gift and a card from someone who hates you.

Does that make the gifts and gestures Loving?
Absolutely not.
Even if it's a musical card.

Which means the gifts and gestures mean absolutely nothing.

Ask yourself:
Do I want to be "romantic" with my partner because I feel I have to be?
Or because a certain time of the year comes around?

Do I want my partner to treat me a certain way only because
They feel pressured to?
Or because they genuinely want to?

Again,
Only do what you want to do, and don't do what you don't want to do.

What about Romantic Relationships?

According to the program,
Romance goes hand-in-hand with an intimate relationship.
It calls this a *"romantic relationship"*.

Remember,
This Manual is about *Love and Loving relationships,*
Not Romantic relationships.

This does not mean that a Loving relationship cannot also be romantic.

The problem comes when the program is attached to a relationship being
A *"romantic relationship"*.

Why does it do this?
The program believes in different "levels" and "kinds" of Love.
The program believes there is a different and "special kind" of Love
To be found in romantic relationships.

So it puts a different value on the "romantic form" of relationships
Than it does other forms of relationships.

CAUTION!!!
It is very dangerous to look at relationships in this way.
Why?
Whenever you compare *anything,*
(People, relationships, partners, etc.)
You are setting up competition,
And competition means what?

It's a game!

Don't play the program's game by comparing relationships.
All relationships are exactly what they are.
They each have their own gifts.
And no relationship is any more or any less special than any other.

How does Love see romantic relationships?

Love sees all relationships the same.
Love does not focus on the form of the relationship you are having.
Love focuses on the content of the relationship.
That content being Loving.

Whether it is a relationship with a family member,
Partner, friend, colleague, etc.
Love only asks one thing in regards to all relationships:

"Is this relationship Loving?"

So if you're dependent on your relationship to be
Riddled with romance in order to have Love –
The Love in your relationship will appear
To fluctuate, and this will cause fear.

Love does not change or fluctuate.
Love is always the same for everyone.

Love is Maximal.

LOVING ROMANCE
Romance in the Service of Love

Like everything else on the level of form,
You *can* use romance in the service of Love.
How?
If you are joining in your Goal and Purpose, which is to Love each other –
Everything you do and say will be given and received as what it is:
Expressions of Love.

Sometimes the expressions of Love may take the form of
Romance and romantic gestures.
This is Beautiful.
Why?
Because it comes from Love,
And Love is Beautiful.

The real questions are:

What is the purpose of our romance?
What is our romance for?
How does our romance serve our Love?

HOPELESS PROMANTICS
Be Aware of the program

Don't get caught up on the program's hype about
Your relationship being "romantic" or not.
Remember, the program ALWAYS chooses form over content.
Why?
Because the program believes the "perfect form"
Will bring you the "perfect content" –
Happiness.

Do not forget that the program is *hopelessly* misguided.

Ever wonder why the program will call YOU "hopeless"
When you are committed to being a "romantic"?

It's telling on *itself* here.

How?
Because the program is Truly a hopeless case.
There is no hope to be found in any form.

Why?

Because no form will deliver the same content to everyone, every time.
Which is why all forms are totally unreliable.

What is the only thing you can rely on a form to do?

Eventually fail you.

Guess what never fails?

Love never fails.

Relationships committed to Love cannot fail.

Again,
Love is not romance –
And romance can be used in the service of Love.

So, regardless of the form your gestures may take,
Always come back to this question:

"Does it come from Love?"

CHAPTER 18
SEX?

Sex Means Absolutely Nothing
You Give Sex All the Meaning It Has To You

Sex is not good or bad, right or wrong, Holy or sinful.
Sex is neutral.
The purpose you give sex is what gives it meaning to you.

The questions to ask are:
Are you having sex in a state of Love or fear?
Are you having sex in a state of guilt or Innocence?
What is the Purpose of your sexual joining? What is it for?

Since sex involves another person, you must join in a mutual goal.
Sex itself may be neutral, but it can be used to hurt or to Heal.
It can be used to express Love or to express fear –
And absolutely nothing in-between.
That is why rape is sex, but it is hurtful. It is not consensual.
Love is always consensual.

The program teaches that sex is special, sex is meaningful, sex is Holy.
Remember,
Sex is nothing.

The goal is always Love.
Love can be expressed in any form, including sex.
Fear can also be expressed in any form, including sex.
Which is why sex should be used as a means of Joining in Love.
If it is not used for Joining in Love, you will use it to hurt yourself.
Do not proceed.

This is a Manual about Love and relationships.
Not sex.
Sexual interplay can be used as a delivery system for expressing
Love, Fun, and Healing in your relationship.
Sex can also be used by the program as a delivery system for
Massive amounts of guilt, fear, upset and pain.

Again, we are discussing **Universal Principles** – form and content.
So whether it's hugging, kissing, texting or talking,
You shouldn't engage in *anything* from a state of fear.

CHAPTER 19
TAKING FULL RESPONSIBILITY
Grown talk

Here is the scene:
Two partners are having a phone conversation in the morning.

Follow this conversation:

[Partner 1 calls partner 2, partner 2 picks up]
Partner 2: "Hello?"
Partner 1: "Good morning."
Partner 2: "Good morning my Love! How are you feeling?"
Partner 1: "Ahhh...I'm actually in pain right now"
Partner 2: [concerned] "Really? What happened?"
Partner 1: "Well, I woke up this morning thinking about you, and on my
       way to the bathroom I banged my foot on the door."
Partner 2: "Wow. That hurts."
Partner 1: [long silence] "Soooooo...I'm waiting."
Partner 2: "Waiting for what?"
Partner 1: "Your apology."
Partner 2: [Shocked] *"Apology for what?"*
Partner 1: "I told you. I'm in pain. My foot hurts."
Partner 2: *"And...*what does that have to do with *me* giving *you* an
       apology?"
Partner 1: "I told you I was thinking about **YOU** when it happened."
Partner 2: [pauses] *"So...*you expect me to ***apologize to you*** for what
       you did to yourself?"
Partner 1: ...
Partner 2: "Bye."

That is about as much sense as the program makes
When it comes to your feelings being hurt.

It is the exact same scenario when your feelings are hurt.
It may not be easy to accept, but it is absolutely True.

TRUTH PRINCIPLE
You Are Responsible for How You Feel At ALL Times

HOW DID YOU MAKE YOURSELF FEEL?
You Are Responsible for Your Feelings

One of the most important things you can do for your relationship is to
Take responsibility for how you feel.

We covered the Truth behind how your feelings work
And where they come from.
When you feel upset for any reason you feel attacked.

Let's take a look at the program's perspective first:

Attack and Defense

Who is really feeling attacked?

The first thing you must realize is that it is never YOU who feels attacked,
It is always the program.
When you feel attacked, you have identified with the program.
When your partner says or does something that
The program (in your mind) doesn't like,
The program feels personally attacked.
Why?
The program has *scripts* for how your partner (and everyone actually)
Should speak and act.
When they do not speak or act in that scripted manner,
The program feels attacked and threatened.

You already know that Love cannot be threatened,
Therefore Love cannot be attacked.
The program on the other hand,
Can be threatened and attacked by anything.

Love is strong.
It needs no protection, and it does not defend itself.
The program is weak.
It feels attacked all the time, and always defends itself.
Sometimes it defends itself by attacking first.
Sometimes it braces for attack and defends its position.
This is playing offense and defense.
Where do you play offense and defense?

In games!

TRUTH PRINCIPLE
Attack Can Only Be Made Upon a Body

Nothing anyone says or does means anything.
YOU give it all the meaning it has.
If someone is not attacking your BODY, they are not attacking you.

Question:
What if they said or did something that was MEANT to be hurtful?

Answer:
*It doesn't matter what **they** meant by it.*
*What matters is the meaning **you** give it.*
Attack can only be made on a body.

Example:
If you take a knife and stab (attack) any*body* with it,
*What will happen to every single **body**?*

They will all bleed.

If you take something someone said or did to *"hurt your feelings"*,
And you say or do the same thing to everyone –
Will everyone react the same?
Will everyone feel hurt by it?

No.

Conclusion:
If what you say or do cannot produce the SAME reaction
In everyone ALL the time,
What was said and what was done mean
ABSOLUTELY NOTHING.
You give it all the meaning it has.

If you feel attacked, it is because you are listening to the program.

The program teaches that your feelings are caused
By people and situations outside of you.
It teaches that you can't help but feel or see certain things in a certain way.

TRUTH PRINCIPLE
You Are Not Responsible for how Your Partner Feels at ANY Time

This may not be an easy Principle to Accept,
But there is power and Freedom in Accepting this.

Why?

Because if you can give something a meaning that will hurt you,
You can also do what?

You can give it a meaning that will give you Peace.

You can change your mind

RELATIONSHIP RESPONSIBILITY
How Does Love and the program look at Responsibility?

Let's take at look at what both the program and Love
Teach about "emotional responsibility" in relationships.

[TABLE ON NEXT PAGE]

EMOTIONAL RESPONSIBILITY

THE PROGRAM TEACHES	LOVE TEACHES
You make me Happy.	*You make yourself Happy.*
If you Love someone, You want to make them Happy.	*If you Love someone, You want to **support** their Happiness.*
You made me upset.	*You made yourself upset.*
If you Love someone, Don't make them upset.	*You are upset because of How you are seeing things. You can choose to see things differently.*
If you changed _____, Things would be better In our relationship.	*If you changed the way You looked at _____, You would realize that our relationship Cannot be threatened by anything. Including _____.*
You hurt my feelings. You made me angry. What you said was hurtful.	*Your feelings are hurt because you are listening to the program. The program hates you. You can choose to listen to Love.*
You complete me. We complete each other.	*You are already Complete. I am already Complete. We join in our Fullness together.*
Arguments are healthy and Show we care about Each other. *Arguing shows we care About our relationship.*	*Arguing shows that you Did not set the goal, And that you are still playing games. An argument is a Competition of inflamed feelings. Competition means **it's a game.***
When you said or did _____, It made me upset.	*You are giving what was said or done all The meaning it has. _____ doesn't mean anything.*

If you Love your partner,
Take responsibility for your feelings.
Take responsibility for how you are *making* yourself feel

Just Tell the Truth
The Solution to Every Problem

How do you stop the program in its tracks?

It's important to know what makes the program seem stronger,
And what makes the program fade and disappear.

What does the program feed on?
The program feeds on attention.

How do you give the program your attention?

You give it attention by focusing on what it's telling you in the moment.

What will happen when you do that?

It will appear to get bigger, stronger, louder, scarier and more real.

Who taught you that focusing on your problems is the solution?

The program.

The program THRIVES on your attention to it.
It tells you that the way you are feeling is your partner's fault.
This is always a lie.

So, why do I get upset?

You don't get upset, the program does.

When you "get upset" it is because you are listening to the program,
And identifying yourself with it.
You chose to listen to its misguidance, and identify yourself as a victim.

YOU ARE NOT A VICTIM.

You are not a victim of your thoughts, or someone else's thoughts.
You are not a victim of your feelings, or someone else's feelings.
You are not a victim of your actions, or someone else's actions.

<u>TRUTH PRINCIPLE</u>
No One can MAKE You Feel Loved
No One can MAKE You Feel fear

How you feel has nothing to do with what your partner does,
Or doesn't do.

Let's be perfectly clear:

No one can hurt your feelings,
And no one can MAKE you feel Love.

How you feel is always YOUR choice.
You have the power of decision.

You do not react to anything directly.
You are always reacting to your OWN interpretation of a neutral event.

Again, nothing means anything.
You give everything all the meaning it has.

This principle is the basis of everything.
This is what will help you perceive everything correctly – with Love.

EMOTIONAL TRIGGERS
How Do Feelings Get Triggered?

Let's examine what the program is teaching you
About your internal experiences, *(also known as)*
Your emotions and feelings, and how they come about.

Let's break this down step-by-step.

The Lie:

1. Something happens.
2. You FEEL either Love or fear.
3. You confuse Step 1 as the cause of step 2.
   a. Since Step 1 and 2 happened almost simultaneously.

Result:
You are now experiencing life as a passive victim of
What's going on around you.
You feel as though people and circumstances have the power
To control your emotions and feelings.
Why?
Because whenever step one happens,
The program wants you to believe it was that (neutral) event
That triggered your feelings.

What if you are experiencing Loving feelings?
It's the same false premise.
You are still disempowering yourself if you think that someone or
Something can MAKE you Happy.
This is just as hazardous to your understanding
As thinking that someone or something can MAKE you angry or fearful.

Now let's take a look at the way Love sees it.

The TRUTH:

1) Something happens.
2) YOU INSTANTLY DECIDE how to perceive it.
   a) Either with Love or fear.

This is the step missing from the program's version of it.
Why?
Because this is the step that puts the power directly back where it belongs:
Back in your hands.

Remember:
You have the Power of Decision.
You can DECIDE to see it RIGHT (with Love),
Or wrong (with fear).

3) You FEEL either Love or fear.

4) It's ok either way. *Why?* Because whether you feel Loving or fearful feelings:
   a) You know that you are innocent.
   b) You know you didn't do anything wrong.
   c) You know that your feelings are just EXPERIENCES.
   d) You allow yourself to FEEL your FEELINGS FULLY.
      i) It's like watching a film or playing a video game.
      ii) If your feelings are not coming from Love (not bringing you Peace), you KNOW they don't mean anything.
         (1) Your unloving feelings shouldn't be taken sincerely, and they shouldn't be taken as a guide for how you should now act or speak.
5) If you are feeling Loving feelings, it's easy –
   a) *You simply carry on.*
6) If you are feeling fearful feelings from the program, you begin to deprogram your thinking.

How?

DEPROGRAMMING

The Purification Process

What Do You Do If You Are Experiencing Unloving (fearful) Feelings?

You already know what to do if you're feeling Love. That's easy.
The question is:
What do you do when the program is running?
This is where you need help.

How do you call on Love to help you?

Remember,
You are not alone. Love is on your side.
You just need to ask.
Then allow.
Allow the Love within you to Guide you.

How do you do this?

First things first...

Check in with yourself!

Ask yourself the question:

"Do I like how I feel right now?"

If the answer is "no", that means the program is running,
Which means that you need to:

STOP!
Just Stop

STOP doing what you're doing.
STOP saying what you're saying.
STOP thinking what you're thinking.

Then take a deep breath

Say to yourself:
I am feeling disturbed.
Whatever I think I am disturbed about doesn't mean anything.
I am giving it all the meaning it has.
How can I see Peace instead of this?
How can I feel Love instead of this?
I am Innocent and so is my partner.
I didn't do anything wrong.
My partner didn't do anything wrong.
I want to join with my partner. I do not want to separate.
I will not allow the program to dictate my actions or my words.
I want to experience Love with my partner,
Now.

This is the Truth.
These are the thoughts of Love.
These are the Loving thoughts you put into your mind and focus on
When the program is giving you fearful thoughts.
These are the thoughts Love wants you to have, all the time.
This is the practical guidance your curriculum offers you
For any situation involving the program.
This is how you call on Love as your Guide.
This is how you take responsibility for your feelings.
This is how you receive the Loving correction of your misperceptions.
This is how you undo fear in your mind and in your relationship.
This is how you undo the program in your mind and in your relationship.
This is how you deprogram yourself.

Here's another question:
How can I AVOID having the program come up in the first place?

Remember, the program is on duty 24/7. It never sleeps.
The program is always looking for an opportunity
To attack you and attack your relationship.
So don't be concerned about if it will come up or not.
Why?

Because it will come.

It will.

Make Peace with that.

Remember the *Purification Process?*
Everything that is not Love WILL come up to be released.

Don't take the program, or anything that comes from it seriously.
The program is just a foolish and delinquent thought system in your mind.

It is totally harmless.

The program cannot hurt you in any way (on its own).
So how do you get hurt?
Listening to its lies is what hurts you.
Following its misguidance is what hurts you.
Remember also that it cannot *help* you in any way.
Choosing to not listen to it anymore is what helps you.

You are now following a curriculum designed to expose the program
In all its forms.
The program does not like being exposed.
It really doesn't.

So what will it do?

It will feel threatened, and it will get very sneaky.
It will still attack your mind with lies,
But it will change its method of attack.

How?

It will sneak attack you.

Why?

It knows you are aware of it now,
And it knows that you recognize its shenanigans,
So it will hide, to protect itself.

When will it come up?
When the Love in your relationship is flowing along smoothly,
It will try to catch you off-guard.

All of a sudden something unexpected happens!

Something is said or done –
And now you find yourself in a state of shock.

You don't know how to see with Love.
You forget all about Love.
And the program starts whispering lies to you.
It wants you to go back to your past learning.

Which is what?

FEAR and GUILT.
Playing the victim role.
Separation.

How to best avoid that though?
Simple.
What you do is this:

Together
SET THE GOAL
At the beginning of each day.
SET THE GOAL
For each situation you find yourselves.
SET THE GOAL
At the beginning of each encounter.
SET THE GOAL
At the beginning of each conversation, call, text, email, etc.
SET THE GOAL
That you will decide to see your partner,
The situation, and whatever comes up at any time,
With Love.

Your Goal is to be Truly Helpful.
Your Goal is to be the Presence of Love.
Love is home in you.
Fear and the program are strangers in you.
Set the goal to see everything correctly.
Set the goal to see everything as Love would see it.

Know that whatever is said,
And whatever appears to be happening:

You are responsible for your feelings about it.

Your feelings are just experiences.

Remember:

Love Celebrates.

*So why not **Celebrate** your experiences?*

First,
Take responsibility for your experience.

It is your power, and it is your privilege.

No one can do this for you.

You are a creator of your experience, not a victim.

If you Love your partner, and you Love yourself –
Set the Goal for Love.

And tell the Truth about the program.

The Truth is NOT a Game.

CHAPTER 20
BEGINNING RELATIONSHIPS?
Are You Totally Fulfilled Without One?

Whether you are in a relationship or not,
This is a good question to ask:

When is the best time to start a relationship?

As you know, the program has an answer for this question,
And so does Love.
Let's see what kind of insanity the program has to say first.

When does the program say you should start a relationship?

According to the program,
You only want to be in a relationship because
You feel a lack within yourself.
You ultimately feel a lack of Love,
And you get in a relationship to fill that lack.
A partner is chosen *only* if you think you can **GET**
The Love you lack from them.
This always entails some kind of *form* and *scripts* for the Love you want.
These are called *"imagined needs"*.

Does it matter who the other person is?
It does not matter who they are,
It only matters what you think you can GET from them.
If they are also operating from the program, they will feel the same way.
Operating from a state of lack,
You will both try to GET the other to give you Love
In the form of your imagined needs.

How does this look?
Since the basis for your relationship is misdirection and deception,
Neither of you will show up honestly and authentically.
You will both put on false personas in order to manipulate the other
Into catering to your imagined needs.
For as long as your strategy works,
You will believe the relationship is a success.

But where do you use strategies?
In games!

When your stratagems no longer work,
You will turn to outright attack, anger and guilt to get what you want.

This ends how?

You guessed it!

Relationship wreck.

What is the program's thinking when entering relationships?

The program enters into all relationships obsessed with these questions:

What can I GET from this relationship?
What can I GET from this person?
How can I GET them to give it to me?

Like a starving savage beast,
It will do whatever is necessary to appease its appetite.

The only problem is, it has an appetite for *imaginary needs,*
And what is imaginary does not exist.
What does not exist is not real,
And what is not real cannot fulfill you.
So why seek for it?

Only Love is real, and Love is already within you.

Never enter into a relationship when you think you need
To get anything from anyone.

Never enter into a relationship when you think
You are incomplete without one.
You can only hurt yourself this way.
You will use the relationship to hurt yourself.

When does Love start Relationships?

Remember Love's simple rule?

"It's only okay if it's okay either way."

Love is totally Happy and Fulfilled with or without a relationship.
Therefore Love Joins in a relationship and with a partner

When does the fear start?

The fear starts before you physically separate,
And continues after you physically separate.

Why do you feel fear?

You feel fear because you don't see them as a partner anymore,
But as an enemy to your Peace.
You see them as your problem.
The program convinces you that the reason
You don't have Peace is because of THEM.
This is the way the program gets you to see them as your adversary.
An adversary is an opponent.
And where do you find opponents?

In games!

What is the source of your problem (your fear)?

The program tells you that your partner is the source of your problem,
And the reason for your fear.
It offers you its typical solution.
It tells you the way to fix this problem is
To remove the source of the problem – your partner.
According to the program,
The only way to have Peace is to "break up" with them.

What does "break up" mean to the program?

The program believes "breaking up" means to "physically separate",
And sever all conceivable connections to them.
If you listen to the program,
It provides you with instructions on how to "break up".

Here are some of its instructions:
- Delete their contact
- Erase their pictures
- Return their gifts
- Get rid of their stuff
- Unfriend them and stop following them on all social media
- Avoid them
- Avoid those people and places associated with them

What is all this?

These are some forms of the *separation ritual*
The program wants you to go through.

Again, they are just forms, so they don't mean anything.
If you are listening to the program while doing these things,
It means you are afraid.

What is the purpose of the separation ritual?
The lie the program tells you is that the purpose of the separation ritual
Is to give you Peace.

What are you really doing?

Absolutely nothing.

Why?

It's not really them that is causing you pain.
You may think that by removing the symbols (forms)
That remind you of them, that you are Healing.
But those are just forms. Forms don't mean anything.
You can remove all the forms associated with them,
But you still have all of the content *you have* associated with them.
Which is what?

Fear.

Subconsciously, you are attempting to separate yourself from
The IDEA of them.

Why?

Because it is the idea of them that is causing you pain, not them.

When you go through the program's separation ritual,
It is always because you are not seeing them correctly.
You are giving yourself fear around the idea of them.
Your thoughts, ideas, memories, experiences, and perceptions of them
Have been poisoned by the program.

That is why you feel pain.

The program wants you to think that when you get rid of them forever –
You will be fine.

But think about it…

You can delete their picture…
But you can't delete the idea of them.

You can erase their contact info…
But you can't erase the time you shared together.

You can return their gifts…
But you can't return the experiences you had together.

You can block their number…
But you can't block the pain you are causing yourself.

You can avoid them…
But you can't avoid the *thought* of them.

You can deny them…
But you can't deny the impact they've had on your life.

So STOP!
Just stop.

How do you Heal?

It's not about removing *them* from your life.

So what is it about?

It's about changing your mind about them.

You already have the tools you need to do that.

Hint:
Read the chapter on forgiveness again

YOU ARE ALWAYS CONNECTED
Relationships Do Not End, They Change Form

When a Loved one dies, do you forget they existed?
Do you simply find someone to replace them?

Let's take a grandparent for example.
Do you just go out and find a "new" grandparent?
No.
Do you stop talking about them?
Do you stop thinking about them?
Do you stop remembering them?
Does your life stop being impacted by them?

No.

This works the same way with everyone.

Your relationships do not end, they simply change form.

<u>REMEMBER LOVE'S PRINCIPLE</u>
You Are Not Your Body

Your partner is not their body either.
You *have* bodies.
The program believes that when your *bodies*
Are no longer together in relationship, neither are you.

Lies!

This would be true if you were *only* a physically embodied being,
But you are a *multidimensional* Being.
What does that mean?

It means you operate on multiple levels simultaneously.

You operate on the physical level because –
You have a body.
You operate on the mental level because –
You have a mind.
You operate on the emotional level because –
You have emotions and feelings.

You *transcend* all conceivable levels because –
You are Love.

As you can see, you exist and operate on *many* different levels,
And only *one* of those levels is physical.

If you ever Loved someone,
You have connected with them on *all* of those other levels.

So what does your physical separation mean to Love?

Absolutely nothing!

Even if you are totally unaware of it,
You are always connected to everyone you encounter.
There's no point in fighting it.

It is not possible to erase every experience,
Every memory, every thought, and every effect
Someone has had on your life.
It is not possible to stop or erase the impact they have had,
Or continue to have on your life experience.
So Stop.

SEPARATING FOR LOVE
Choose To See Them Correctly

Here's a question:
"What if I no longer WANT to be physically connected to them?"

Love is Freedom.

Remember?
Always do what you want to do,
And don't do what you don't want to do.

You don't ever have to see them, speak to them,
Or follow them on Instagram again if you don't want to.

The questions to ask are:
What is the Purpose of our separation?

What is it for?
How are we using separation to support our Goal,
Which is Love?

Just as Love uses joining for its Purpose,
Love can use separation for a Loving Purpose.

How?

If you are in a relationship where both you and your partner
Continue to use the relationship to hurt yourselves,
It's time to separate for Love.

Remember what your relationship and your joining is for.
It is for Healing your emotional wounds.
If physical joining in your relationship is used to deepen your wounds –
You are not meeting your Goal.
When joining is not helpful to your Goal and Purpose,
It's time to change the form of your relationship.

Changing form *CAN* include physical separation.

What should you do first?

Ask for Love's Guidance.

You should only do what the Love within you *Guides* you to do.

If Love Guides you to separate, its Purpose is always:

Separation to Heal.

There is no judgment, attack, condemnation, or grievances involved.
There is no attachment to any specific outcome.

If you are listening to the program, you are separating out of fear.
Which means you are attached to a specific outcome,
Even if that specific outcome is "never seeing them again".

The program believes your Peace lies in form,
Including the form of the separation.

Love understands that forms change.
Love is not attached to any specific form.

Just as the form of physical separation can be used to Heal –
Love remains open to Heal in other ways.

So, if you don't want to join right now,
That doesn't mean you hate them.
That doesn't mean you don't care about them.
That doesn't mean you have fear about them.

What does it mean?

The purpose of your separation determines the meaning.

<u>**LOVE PRINCIPLE**</u>
Only Loving Thoughts Are True

You can still have Loving thoughts,
Loving feelings,
Loving words,
And Loving perceptions about anyone –
Regardless of the current form of your relationship with them.

Just Remember:

Your unloving thoughts and feelings about anyone
Always hurt YOU.

Your Loving thoughts and feelings about anyone
Always serve EVERYONE.

If you want your relationship to heal,

Remember Love.

EPILOGUE
Stop Wasting Time

Stop acting like tomorrow is promised to you, or to anyone.

It isn't.

There is only one thing in life that is certain.

What is that?

The fact that you will die.

Your partner will die.
Everyone you know will die,
And everyone you don't know will die.
This is certain.
The only thing that is uncertain is...

When?

Have this Conversation

YOU HAVE 24 HOURS
Plenty of Time to Express Love

Here is your final assignment:

Check the time.
Whatever time it is right now,
Give yourself and your partner 24 hours to live.

Ask your partner:
"What would you want to do if this was our last 24 hours?"

Be present.
Be deliberate.
Be sincere, not serious.
Have fun with it.
Do it.
NOW.

Ask yourself:
Is there something left unsaid?
Say it.
Is there something left undone?
Do it.
Is there something you have been meaning to express?
Express it.
Is there a question you've been meaning to ask?
Ask it.

Start Now!
If you don't start today, you won't finish tomorrow.
Tomorrow is not promised.
Really, *today* is not promised.

When does Love operate?

Love operates right now.

The program wants you to think that you have time.
Time to figure it out. Time to figure them out.
Love knows better.
Love doesn't waste any time figuring anything or anyone out.
Why?
Because you can skip the whole process of trying to figure out,
When you simply:

Accept and Appreciate.

You can Accept your partner Fully
Without having to understand them Fully.
You can Appreciate your partner Fully
Without having to figure them out Fully.

Appreciate. Appreciate. Appreciate.

Only you have the power to express your Love and your Appreciation.
It's easy to Appreciate your partner, and it's easy to forget to.

Do it.

No one will express your Love and Appreciation for you.

When is the right time to Appreciate?

Right now.

Appreciation is always right on time.

Do not fall for the program's lies that you can *get around to it.*

There is no getting around to Love and Appreciation.

Do it.

If you don't do it,
Who will?

If you don't do it now,
When will you?

If you don't do it here,
Where will you?

Stop wasting time.

Ask yourself:

"If I had 24 hours left to live,
Would I waste that time worrying about
Whatever I'm worrying about right now?

If I had 24 hours left to live,
Would I entertain the program's madness for another 5 seconds?

If I had 24 hours left to live,
What would I do?"

Once Again:

The purpose of this Manual is for you to have an experience –

To Inspire you
To give yourself
The EXPERIENCE of Love.

Are you done?

Just because you have reached the final page of this Manual –

Don't think that you're done.

You are not done.
You have just begun.

This is a Manual for Loving Relationships –

Have one!

The Time for Love is Now.

&

IS *NOT* A
GAME

Thanks for reading.

…To be continued.